Praise for *Every Guest is a Hero*

Want a great way to view Disney theme parks? *Every Guest is a Hero* provides a unique lens—Joseph Campbell's pioneering work on storytelling—that helps explain just how and why the parks continue to exert such a hold on audiences worldwide. After reading this book, you will see the parks in a new light.

> Melody Malmberg, author of *Walt Disney Imagineering: A Behind the Dreams Look at Making MORE Magic Real* and *The Making of Disney's Animal Kingdom Theme Park*

A fascinating look at a theme park guest's journey and a great foundation for any fan of Disney storytelling.

> Anthony Esparza, Senior VP, Guest Experiences, Design & Development, Herschend Family Entertainment

Every successful Disney attraction and themed environment is built from a recipe using the timeless elements of storytelling that have bound humanity together for eons. Walt Disney knew how to do this intuitively, taught his designers how to do it, and now you will be let in on the secret. Adam Berger brings together the observations of Joseph Campbell and applies them to the world of the theme park, forever changing the way we perceive those magical places.

> Sam Gennawey, author of *The Disneyland Story: The Unofficial Guide to the Evolution of Walt Disney's Dream* and *Walt and the Promise of Progress City*

Adam Berger's analysis of storytelling in Disney's theme parks is an amazing journey into the creative thought process at Walt Disney Imagineering. It is what attraction designers hope for as an understanding of their product, and wish for in a guest's experience.

> Trevor Bryant, Creative Director, BB Productions

EVERY GUEST IS A
HERO

Disney's Theme Parks *and the*
Magic of Mythic Storytelling

Adam M. Berger

PRESS

To Julia, my beloved muse

PREFACE
How to use this book

MOST VISITORS TO DISNEY'S THEME PARKS find they are able to enjoy the parks on several levels. Depending on your outlook and mood, your Disney theme park visit may be all about fun or thrills or nostalgia...or maybe you're seeking an uplifting infusion of laughter, enchantment, and wonder. Yet there are other levels to the Disney parks and attractions that may not be so obvious, though they play a major role in your guest experience. *Every Guest is a Hero* will help you recognize and appreciate some of these hidden levels, adding a new dimension of enjoyment to your visits.

But please don't take this book into the parks with you and go around analyzing everything—especially if it's your first visit. (And first time visitors beware: this book is loaded with spoilers.) Instead, I hope you will take the opportunity to relax and enjoy the Disney parks as they are meant to be enjoyed: as pleasurable, entertaining, and often exciting experiences. As you go, you may want to make mental notes about which parts of your visit are most enjoyable. What are the high points? Which attractions or other features seem to connect with you emotionally or otherwise produce some degree of psychological impact?

After you get home, you can open this book and embark on your adventure through the world of Disney's mythic storytelling to discover how and why those experiences produced such strong emotional responses. Then, the next time you visit a Disney theme park, you may find that you are able to enjoy the experience in a whole new way. And that, ultimately, is the whole point of this book.

Adam M. Berger
Orlando, Florida
November, 2013

TABLE OF CONTENTS

INTRODUCTION

Decoding Disney's theme parks

ENTER ANY DISNEY THEME PARK and chances are you'll find yourself feeling curiously uplifted. Within minutes, you may notice your capacity for wonder engaged and your appetite for adventure heightened. Novel sights, sounds, and aromas engulf your senses. Compelling attractions beckon you to explore exotic jungles, far-flung worlds, and fantastic locales teaming with pirates, princesses, dinosaurs, and "999 happy haunts."

Other things—a fleet of vintage steam locomotives, characters from your favorite Disney movies—seem familiar and even nostalgic. Yet these encounters also appear somehow fresh and different and exciting. Before you know it, you may feel as though you've been conveyed into another realm as the everyday concerns and priorities of the "ordinary world" outside the park fade into the background. You may even feel yourself not just transported, but somehow…transformed.

What is going on here?!!

What's so special about a Disney theme park? What separates the Disney experience from the experiences in your everyday life…or the experiences you will find in a typical regional amusement park, for that matter? Is it the clever costumes and imaginative architecture? The evocative lighting and appealing background music? The entertaining characters and ingenious shows and rides? The meticulous attention to detail and Disney's renowned commitment to cleanliness and customer service?

Actually, it's all of the above. But there is also something more subtle at work. It's so subtle, in fact, it's easily overlooked—even though it's in your face virtually every moment of your Disney theme park experience.

That subtle something, of course, is *storytelling*.

The Walt Disney Company's mastery of storytelling has always been the hallmark of its entertainment products—originally on the theater screen, then later on television, and ultimately in its theme parks, where the storytelling becomes three-dimensional and immersive.

The stories you encounter in the Disney parks are conveyed in many different forms, through different mediums and different genres. They are told through thrill rides such as Expedition Everest and Tower of Terror...through "dark rides" such as Haunted Mansion and DINOSAUR...through water-based adventures such as Pirates of the Caribbean and Jungle Cruise...through simulator rides such as Star Tours: The Adventures Continue and Mission: SPACE...and through Audio-Animatronic shows such as The American Adventure, and nighttime spectacles such as Fantasmic! It's even conveyed through the park architecture, landscaping, and the area master plan (the physical arrangement of the entire park).

Once you become aware of the storytelling going on all around you, it may seem as though you are encountering many different stories. And, in fact, you are. Yet, in the most important sense, these numerous stories actually turn out to be *one single story* expressed in many variations through many different formats and mediums.

But this single unifying story is not just some ordinary tale. In fact, it is a powerful mythological story—a "monomyth"—that has been told and retold in endless variations in every culture over countless generations since the dawn of human communication. Those who study this ancient monomyth know it as "the Hero's Journey." It's a metaphor that describes a journey of transformation shared by everyone, everywhere. It resonates with the human psyche in remarkable ways because it embodies the transformative events—the challenges, setbacks, and triumphs—that we all face in life. As a result, the Hero's Journey connects with people of all ages and all backgrounds on a deeply satisfying emotional level.

The Hero's Journey is special, yet you'll find it in the structure and characters of virtually every coherent story if you look for it. Some stories feature the Hero's Journey more explicitly than others, including those contained in the most popular motion pictures, television shows, stage dramas, musicals, and literary works.

When the Hero's Journey is employed skillfully, it can work box office magic. You'll find the elements of the Hero's Journey at the core of some of the most successful motion pictures of all time, including all of Disney's most popular movies—from *Snow White* and *Pinocchio* to *The Lion King* and *Monsters University.*

While the Hero's Journey can add psychological heft to a movie, the effect can be even more potent in the three dimensional environment of a Disney theme park, where the story surrounds and engulfs you. And just as those hit movies tend to lure high numbers of repeat viewers, the Disney parks attract impressive numbers of returning visitors.

Because of the immersive nature of the Disney theme park experience, you cannot be a passive observer when you are in the parks. Instead, you become an active participant in the story. You are in the middle of the action, exposed to all the story's wonders, dangers, and thrills. In fact, you have not only become one of the characters in the story; you are the story's *hero,* and the mythic adventure is now *your* adventure.

If you are like most guests, chances are you're not consciously aware of the deep psychological currents swirling around you whenever you wade into a Disney theme park. You may sense that something remarkable is happening to you, but you probably can't identify what it is. No problem; the Disney parks are carefully designed to be fun for everyone, and having an awareness of the subconscious forces involved in the experience is not required.

Then again, since you are reading this book, it's probably safe to assume that you are curious to know what's going on below the surface of the guest experience. And that is the reason this book exists: to give you the insight you'll need to recognize the Hero's Journey in all its many incarnations and to enable you to decipher the "mythic source code" that is hidden in plain sight throughout every Disney theme park.

The following chapters will introduce the pattern (the "paradigm") of this ancient story and the assorted symbolic characters (the "archetypes") that typically populate it. You'll then discover how the artists and technical wizards of Walt Disney Imagineering have ingeniously translated these mythic elements into three-dimensional immersive experiences. Then, in the final section, you'll find a collection of "Mything in Action" case studies that examine several popular Disney attractions, taking you on a scene-by-scene exploration of their mythic content.

The Call to Adventure has been sounded. The First Threshold awaits. So strap yourself in, keep your arms and legs inside at all times, and let the Journey begin!

PART I
THE MAGICAL MYTH STORY TOUR

Chapter 1:

Tale as Old as Time

How myths explain us to ourselves

IN THE LABYRINTHINE CAVERNS of Disneyland's Matterhorn Bobsleds, brave Theseus, half-son of Poseidon, hurtles ever closer to his fateful encounter with the Minotaur...which today bears an uncanny resemblance to the legendary Abominable Snowman. Nearby, along the subterranean canals of Pirates of the Caribbean, the Maori hero Māui, in the guise of Captain Jack Sparrow, is poised once again to steal the secret flame of the heavens—this time in the form of the hidden treasure of Puerto Dorado—as the fire goddess Mahuia and her minions (portrayed by Captain Hector Barbossa and his scurvy crew) prepare to unleash their terrible wrath.

On the opposite side of the continent, beneath the blazing Florida sun, Odysseus and his stalwart crew endure a drenching whitewater rafting adventure as they encounter the descendants of the monsters Scylla and Charybdis, who jealously guard the Kali River Rapids at Disney's Animal Kingdom. Not to be outdone, the Norse trickster god Loki has arrived in Tomorrowland at the Magic Kingdom, where he has taken on the form of a cuddly blue space alien and is merrily wreaking all manner of mischief and mayhem in Stitch's Great Escape.

Throughout every visit you make to a Disney theme park, you are constantly immersed in a succession of timeless myths that have been cleverly Imagineered into captivating environments and attractions, always delivered with Disney's trademark flair for storytelling and showmanship. They are made-up stories that resonate in your modern-day subconscious to produce a nearly limitless range of genuine feelings—from anticipation and surprise to giddy terror and wide-eyed wonder.

Myths engage your imagination and your emotions because they embody the fundamental hopes, dreams, fears, and aspirations that all people share. They are metaphors for the human condition...or as some mythologists like to put it: "A myth is a lie that tells the truth." Mythic stories make it possible to encounter big truths about being human and experience them on a personal scale, cloaked in the symbolic language of characters, settings, and situations with which everyone can identify. And one of the most powerful and pervasive expressions of mythic storytelling is the Hero's Journey, which provides a narrative framework upon which all other mythic themes can be arrayed.

The late mythologist, author, and lecturer Joseph Campbell was the first to identify and describe the Hero's Journey, popularizing it through influential books such as *The Hero with a Thousand Faces, The Transformations of Myth through Time,* and *The Masks of God.* He spent much of his career studying and comparing the myths, legends, folk stories and fairy tales of cultures around the world. In doing so, he realized that they all had certain elements in common. The monomyth that Professor Campbell called "the Hero's Journey" is the product of his synthesis of these elements into a universal model or "paradigm." He recognized that all stories told throughout history and across all cultures are expressions of the Hero's Journey, because the Hero's Journey is really the story of all humans everywhere.

In his writings and lectures, Campbell explained how the Hero's Journey resonates with the human psyche and how its major movements—Separation, Descent, Ordeal, and Return—metaphorically echo the key transformations in our own lives: we come into the world helpless and dependent on our parents, who may make many sacrifices for our sakes; we gradually become self-reliant as we cross a succession of thresholds separating childhood dependency from adult responsibility; we face challenges that shape our character and outlook such as school, sports, work, and family life, meeting allies (and sometimes enemies) along the way. Some of us may embark on life-changing quests in pursuit of education, career, marriage, and parenthood. Some may serve in public office, some may fight to defend their country, and some may volunteer to help those in need. And we may ultimately make personal sacrifices for the benefit of others, bringing the adventure that is our lives full circle.

"When we quit thinking primarily about ourselves and our own self-preservation, we undergo a truly heroic transformation of consciousness," Campbell explained. "And what all the myths have to deal with is transformations of consciousness of one kind or another. You have been thinking one way; you now have to think a different way." Yet even though many of these key life cycle events may not apply to everyone's life story, the inner transformations they inspire are nevertheless deeply embedded in our collective psyche.

While the "Mythic Round" of the Hero's Journey symbolically represents the stages of the human life cycle, it also plays into the individual events, large and small, of our daily lives. We embark on a Hero's Journey when we enroll in a new school…when we learn to ride a bicycle…when we join a sports team…when we are faced with a medical crisis…when we go job-hunting…when we bring a child into the world. We are *always* in the midst of a Hero's Journey. It's one of the things that make us human, and it's the reason we respond so readily when we find the Hero's

Journey creatively presented in a novel, on a theater stage, on a television or movie screen…or in a theme park.

Early in his career, Campbell's observations were of interest mostly within academic circles, though they began to attract broader public attention with the publication of his book *The Hero with a Thousand Faces* in 1949. His work achieved mainstream notice in the late 1970s when the screenwriter and movie director George Lucas revealed that Campbell's books were a major source of inspiration for his cinematic *Star Wars* saga. Later, in a video interview with journalist Bill Moyers, Lucas summarized the importance of myths in our daily lives. "Myths help you to have your own Hero's Journey, find your individuality, find your place in the world," Lucas explained. "But hopefully [myths] remind you that you're part of a whole and that you must also be part of the community above the welfare of yourself."

Shortly before his death in 1987, Campbell recorded a series of far-ranging video dialogues with Moyers, which later aired on PBS. *The Power of Myth* broadcasts, along with a best-selling companion transcript volume, brought Campbell's insights into the Hero's Journey and the impact of mythology on everyone's daily lives to an even wider audience. Today, screenwriters and directors are consciously integrating the Hero's Journey paradigm and character archetypes into their movies. Like George Lucas, they discovered that the psychological allure of the Hero's Journey, when handled with skill and sensitivity, could translate into breathtaking box office numbers.

Few showmen have been able to harness the power of the Hero's Journey as consistently and effectively as Walt Disney, even though there is no evidence that he was aware of the monomyth or had ever heard of Joseph Campbell and his works. Walt's mastery of the Hero's Journey, as demonstrated in his numerous hit movies, his popular television programs, and his creation of Disneyland Park, reveals his intrinsic gift for mythic storytelling. He possessed an uncanny ability to view his own work through the eyes of his audience, and therefore recognized which elements of his stories would emotionally connect with them. He understood his audiences' tastes in entertainment because they were *his* tastes.

In designing Disneyland, Walt realized that his guests would naturally personalize their adventures, making them their own. He knew that they would not only enter the stories told at Disneyland (and in other Disney theme parks yet to be conceived), but would themselves become the heroes of those stories. He even hinted at this sense of personal ownership in the speech he gave on the park's opening day on July 17, 1955. Walt's words are memorialized on a plaque that is permanently mounted at the base of the flagpole in Disneyland's Main Street Square. It begins:

To all who come to this happy place: Welcome.
Disneyland is your land.

The Hero's Journey forms the narrative foundation of every Disney theme park—from Anaheim to Hong Kong (and soon Shanghai)—and all the experiences within them. By mastering the mythic energy of the Hero's Journey, the Imagineers who design the Disney parks and attractions wield a powerful creative tool that enables them to emotionally connect with you and your fellow guests in ways both sublime and profound, enticing you to return again and again.

In the following chapters, we will explore the many ways in which the Hero's Journey is manifested within the parks as we decipher the mythic source code of the Disney guest experience. But first, we need to familiarize ourselves with the stages of the Journey and the archetypal characters who populate it.

Since the motion picture is a familiar storytelling medium through which the Hero's Journey metaphor can be easily examined, we'll use scenes from a spectrum of classic Disney movies to look at the stages of the Journey and its character archetypes, exploring the mythic realm in two dimensions before we move on to the three-dimensional immersive settings of the Disney theme parks.

Chapter 2:

What a Bunch of Characters

Meet the mythic archetypes

THE HERO OF THE HERO'S JOURNEY and all the characters she[1] encounters in the course of the story function as "archetypes," which is the term the Swiss psychologist Carl Jung used to describe characters or entities that reappear time after time in everyone's dreams and in the mythologies of every culture. Jung believed that these different archetypes represent the various aspects of our own personalities. Thus, whenever the hero meets any of these archetypes in the course of her adventure, she is actually encountering a personification of one facet of her own personality. Her adventure will be successfully concluded when she is able to control and integrate all these archetypes to create a complete, mature identity.

One way to look at the mythic archetypes is to picture them as "masks" worn by the characters in the story. A character may wear a single "mask" through the entire Journey, or may switch masks to serve the purposes of the story. The same masks may even get passed around to different characters at various points in the course of the adventure...or a single character may wear multiple masks at the same time (a mentor may also be a threshold guardian, for example). But for now, we'll acquaint ourselves with the most common archetypes one-by-one. They are:

---

[1] Throughout this book, the word "hero" is used to refer to both male and female characters. The alternating use of the masculine and feminine pronouns reflects this duality.

HERO

The hero is the protagonist, the story's central character, and therefore the one who is making the Journey. The hero's role, at its most elemental, is one of service and self-sacrifice, placing the safety and welfare of others above her own. Psychologically, the hero symbolizes the ego (what the Austrian psychoanalyst Sigmund Freud defined as the "I" — the sense of personal identity that distinguishes each of us from everyone else in the world). As mentioned above, the ultimate goal of the hero's quest is to bring together all the different components of the ego (represented by the other archetypes) to achieve a fully rounded sense of self.

The hero's adventure may center on an external quest — a mission to the Special World to restore order and balance to the hero's Ordinary World, as when Simba goes into exile in the lush jungle where he matures and prepares for his fateful return to Pride Rock...or when Sheriff Woody seeks to rescue Buzz Lightyear from sadistic Sid's bedroom. In other stories, the hero may embark on an internal quest in pursuit of true love and self-fulfillment, as when Cinderella decides to attend the royal ball...or the mission may be in search of healing and personal growth, as when Mr. Banks finally internalizes the lessons of Mary Poppins to re-order the priorities in his life.

MENTOR

The mentor provides the wisdom and guidance that the hero will need in order to navigate and overcome the obstacles and challenges awaiting her in the

Special World. On a psychological level, the mentor archetype symbolizes the higher self—the wiser, nobler aspect of our personalities.

As a motivating force, the mentor may provide the hero with knowledge, insight, and training, as when Baloo shows Mowgli how to enjoy "the bare necessities of life" ...or when Belle instructs the Beast in matters of compassion, humanity, and civilized behavior. The mentor may also equip the hero with magical gifts such as weapons, tools, or articles of clothing, as when the Fairy Godmother gives Cinderella an enchanted coach, an elegant ball gown, and other items...or when Peter Pan sprinkles Wendy and her brothers with pixie dust so they can fly to Neverland.

THRESHOLD GUARDIAN

As the title implies, the role of the threshold guardian is to prevent access to the Special World, admitting only those who can prove themselves deserving. Psychologically, the threshold guardian symbolizes our own self-doubts, inner demons, or other negative energies—the neuroses that test our readiness to face the challenges in our lives and to accept the life-altering changes that may result from our personal journeys.

By placing obstacles in the hero's way, the threshold guardian tests the hero's worthiness and commitment to the quest while excluding posers and wannabes. Thus, in *Aladdin*, the (literal) mouth of the Cave of Wonders warns away anyone who's not "...a diamond in the rough," while in *Sleeping Beauty* the towering wall of thorns conjured by Maleficent blocks Prince Phillip's path to the castle where Princess Aurora awaits his awakening kiss.

HERALD

When challenges are declared or crucial changes are on the way, these momentous events are announced to the hero by the herald. In psychological terms, the herald represents the inner voice that informs us that the time has come to make a change in our lives.

The herald issues the Call to Adventure that gets the Hero's Journey rolling, as when the Blue Fairy challenges Pinocchio to prove himself brave, unselfish, and able to tell right from wrong...or when Bert announces the impending arrival of Mary Poppins. The herald also signals significant obstacles or forthcoming trials, as when Maurice's horse Phillipe alerts Belle to her father's plight as a captive of the Beast...or the Great Prince gives Bambi the tragic news that "Your mother can't be with you any more," signaling a new phase in the fawn's life.

SHAPESHIFTER

Sometimes a shapeshifter is able to literally change his or her physical appearance (think of the Wicked Queen in *Snow White*), but more often it's the character's true nature, objectives, or loyalties that are being disguised in order to mislead, confuse, or otherwise thwart the hero (as Cruella de Vil did in *101 Dalmations*). Psychologically, the shapeshifter embodies either the male elements that exist in the female unconscious, which Carl Jung called the "animus," or the female elements in the male unconscious, which Jung called the "anima." For this reason, the shapeshifter character will often (though not always) be the opposite sex of the story's hero...although the hero herself may sometimes wear the shapeshifter "mask."

In *Swiss Family Robinson*, the sea captain's rescued "grandson" turns out to be a girl, with the revelation triggering a sudden rivalry between the boys Fritz and Ernst. And in *Monsters, Inc.* Henry J. Waternoose, III portrays himself as a caring, benevolent boss, but turns out to be a ruthless scoundrel who will stop at nothing to protect his personal interests.

SHADOW

Every hero needs an opponent, foe, antagonist, or archenemy. The shadow serves this important function, driving the conflict at the heart of the story. This archetype also serves the psychological function of embodying our darker impulses, fears, and desires, or our repressed feelings of guilt, regret, or resentment—feelings that threaten to hold us back from our full potential and may even bring about our personal downfall.

In the Hero's Journey, the shadow may be manifested in the form of a monstrously bad person...or an actual monster. Destructive people, monsters, and other figures abound in *Pinocchio*, including the violent puppet maestro Stromboli, the unnamed sinister coachman, and Monstro the whale. In some stories, the shadow may actually be a friend or loved one of the hero—someone who perhaps means well, but whose personal prejudices, preconceptions, or protective instincts stand between the hero and her goal. In Disney's *Tarzan*, for example, the gorilla patriarch Kerchak is a disapproving and even threatening presence in the title character's life (soon to be supplanted in that role by the murderously ambitious hunter-guide Clayton).

TRICKSTER

The trickster character takes delight in unleashing chaos and mischief, disrupting the status quo and forcing change. Tricksters point out folly and hypocrisy wherever they find it, bringing the hero (and sometimes the shadow) down to earth and setting matters into their proper perspective. Psychologically, the trickster represents our own impulse to resist conformity or challenge authority.

Lumiere, Cogsworth, and the other castle staff prove themselves master tricksters as they thwart the attack by Gaston and his mob, and they also turn out to be adept foils to Beast's ponderous self-absorption and gloominess. Stitch's antics force Lilo to become more responsible so she can better appreciate the efforts of her older sister Nani to keep their family together. And Mary Poppins is "practically perfect" when it comes to confounding Mr. Banks' preconceptions and misguided intentions while also beguiling the children.

There are other archetypal figures that show up from time to time—the lost father...the captive princess...the neighborhood eccentric...the gadget guru...the scoundrel with a heart of gold—but most of these tend to be variations, subsets, or offshoots of the primary archetypes. How do these characters fit into the overall adventure in the Mythic Round? We'll find out at our next stop.

Chapter 3:

Ding-dong! Adventure Calling!

The stages of the Hero's Journey

NOW THAT WE HAVE MET the character archetypes that populate the Hero's Journey, the time has come to examine the discrete stages of the Journey that comprise the major movements of *Separation, Descent, Ordeal,* and *Return.*[2]

Although the Hero's Journey often takes the protagonist (and the audience) on a physical journey, the Mythic Round is first and foremost an emotional or

---

[2] The term "movement" is used here in much the same way as it is used to describe a major section of a symphonic work or concerto, with each movement being a self-contained musical work, yet also a part of a larger musical expression.

psychological voyage. It's an inner journey of personal transformation in which the hero will be challenged to grow in character, take individual responsibility, and successfully bring together the different elements of his personality to become an emotionally complete person.

The stages of the Hero's Journey are not set in stone. In fact, they are very flexible, depending on the story being told. The narrative structure can branch off in different directions depending on whether the story is a comedy or a drama. Additional stages can be added, or stages can be subtracted, or the sequence of the stages can be switched around to meet the needs of the story (there may be numerous threshold crossings and several Inmost Caves, for example). A story may contain several complete Hero's Journeys...or the entire story may focus on only a few key stages. For the moment, however, let's acquaint ourselves with the movements and stages of the Hero's Journey in their typical sequence. They are:

1st MOVEMENT: SEPARATION

THE ORDINARY WORLD
The story typically begins in the Ordinary World, where the hero is introduced in his familiar surroundings, setting up a contrast with the Special World to come. Yet even though the Journey may not have officially started, the source of the challenges and conflicts to be encountered in the Special World may already be present and the audience may learn what is at stake. In *Mary Poppins*, the Ordinary World in the Banks household is one of domestic turmoil for which young Jane and Michael are inevitably blamed. In *Beauty and the Beast*, Belle's Ordinary World is one in which she feels restless and

confined, prompting her to sing, *"There must be more than this provincial life!"*

CALL TO ADVENTURE

The story is set into motion when something happens that upsets the harmony or balance of the hero's Ordinary World and requires action to set it right. It may occur on a very personal level, or it could be something that affects the entire community. The Call to Adventure may be the disruptive event itself, or the Call may be delivered by the herald, the mentor, or one of the other character archetypes. The Blue Fairy, for example, is both herald and mentor when she challenges Pinocchio to prove himself brave, unselfish, and able to tell right from wrong by listening to his conscience. The Blue Fairy issues another Call to Adventure later in the story, when she directs Pinocchio to rescue Geppetto from the stomach of Monstro the whale. Early in *The Incredibles*, Bob Parr receives his Call in the form of a mysterious, self-destructing data tablet, which persuades the retired crime fighter to don his Mr. Incredible super-suit once again and embark on a new mission.

REFUSAL OF THE CALL

Often, the Call to Adventure seems too threatening or challenging for the hero, who may doubt (if only briefly) his own abilities. Hence, the Refusal of the Call, as when Wendy initially finds several excuses for not accompanying Peter Pan to Neverland, or when Mowgli refuses to accompany Bagheera to the "man village." In *Monsters, Inc.*, Mike Wazowski refuses to leave the Himalayan ice cavern to search for a portal back to Monstropolis, telling Sulley, "If you want to go out there and freeze to death, you be my guest...because you're on your own."

MEETING WITH THE MENTOR

The mentor has been on this journey before or may have special insight or advice for the hero, helping him gain the fortitude to accept the Call to Adventure, or providing the guidance he will need in order to navigate the unaccustomed landscape of the Special World. Lilo, nominally the hero of *Lilo & Stitch*, temporarily dons the mask of the mentor as she instructs Stitch in the meaning of the word *"'ohana,"* thus preparing the little alien for his own Hero's Journey. In another time and place, Pocahontas is counseled by the arboreal spirit mentor known as "Grandmother Willow," who tells her to listen to her heart.

2nd MOVEMENT: DESCENT

CROSSING THE FIRST THRESHOLD

The First Threshold marks the transition from the Ordinary World to the Special World. In crossing this threshold, the hero signals his commitment to the Journey ahead, with all its dangers and rewards. Additional thresholds may await the hero within the Special World, each one bringing him closer to the object of his quest. Multiple thresholds are crossed, for instance, when Lady is chased by street dogs into unfamiliar territory, and is then escorted by Tramp to the zoo and then around town, introducing her to a world beyond her sheltered existence. Buzz Lightyear and Sheriff Woody, meanwhile, cross the threshold from Andy's bedroom to the world beyond Andy's house, soon finding themselves stranded in the alien realm of a local gas station (and later in the more explicitly alien world of the Pizza Planet restaurant).

THE ROAD OF TRIALS

Before the hero can successfully navigate the Special World, he must first learn the rules of the realm, prepare for the challenges ahead, and gain confidence in his abilities while the stakes grow higher. This is when tests, allies, and enemies come into play. Joseph Campbell referred to this stage of the Journey as "the Road of Trials." This is the point in the Journey when Nemo's dad, Marlin the clownfish, encounters allies such as Dory and Crush...enemies, such as Bruce the shark and his toothy pals...and tests such as the encounter with the stinging jellies. Mary Poppins, meanwhile, constantly tests Mr. Banks' capacity for empathy and whimsy, while Mr. Banks' employers challenge his commitment to his job at the expense of his family life.

APPROACH TO THE INMOST CAVE

Whether the Inmost Cave is a fortified castle, a dark attic, or an actual cave, it is the place where the hero's courage and commitment are put to their greatest test so far. The Approach to the Inmost Cave, therefore, is the time when final preparations are made before the hero must face his greatest fears or most daunting challenge. And so, accompanied by a reluctant Jiminy Cricket, Pinocchio ties a weight to his donkey tail and plunges beneath the waves in search of the whale Monstro. Hitching a ride into deep space, WALL-E follows EVE's scout ship to the *Axiom* and then makes his way to the bridge, picking up important clues about life aboard the giant spaceship along the way.

3rd MOVEMENT: ORDEAL

SUPREME ORDEAL

The hero finally confronts the object of the crisis, facing his deepest fears and tackling his greatest challenge. This Supreme Ordeal is the pivotal point in the Journey. The hero is in enemy territory, the stakes are high, and the risks seem overwhelming. The hero may even be expected to make the ultimate sacrifice, suffering either his own (literal or symbolic) death, or witnessing the death of a mentor or other close ally. In *The Jungle Book*, Baloo and Bagheera team up for a joint Supreme Ordeal as they infiltrate the ruined temple of King Louis to rescue Mowgli. In *Toy Story*, Sheriff Woody makes his way into Sid's creepy bedroom to rescue Buzz Lightyear.

REWARD

Having survived the Supreme Ordeal, the hero either rightfully receives his Reward...or takes it by theft. Either way, the Journey is far from over. Thus, in the forest, John Smith wins Pocahontas' love, not realizing that their supposedly secret rendezvous has been observed by both the settler Thomas and the jealous tribal warrior Kocoum. Over on Syndrome's island, Mr. Incredible reunites with his family...but Syndrome has already set his maniacal scheme in motion.

4th MOVEMENT: RETURN

THE ROAD BACK

After the hero has taken his Reward, the Journey still must be completed, which means he must return to the Ordinary World. But the Road Back is a perilous one, and hostile forces may be in hot pursuit. Such is the case when Monstro, enraged by Pinocchio and Geppetto's escape from his belly, pursues them into a rocky cove, where Pinocchio sacrifices himself to push Geppetto to safety. Likewise, having rescued Boo from Randall Boggs and Mr. Waternoose, Mike and Sulley embark on a desperate race for freedom through the vast Monsters, Inc. door vault.

RESURRECTION

On the Road Back, the hero may face one final life-or-death confrontation, which will prove that he has absorbed the lessons of his journey. The hero may even give up his own life—either figuratively or literally—and then be reborn in order to return to the Ordinary World. The hero may experience "death" directly or vicariously through the loss of a close ally. Such scenes abound in the plots of Disney movies—from *Snow White* to *WALL-E*. They occur with equal frequency in Disney's animated features (Belle's confession of her love for the Beast brings him back to life and lifts the enchantress' curse from him and the entire castle staff) and the studio's live-action films (after being sacked by his employers, Mr. Banks remembers Mary Poppins' talismanic phrase "supercalifragilisticexpialidocious" and realizes that the center of his life is his family, not his workplace.)

RETURN TO THE ORDINARY WORLD

After successfully navigating the Special World, surviving the ordeals, and conquering "death," it is now time for the hero to cross the final threshold and re-enter the Ordinary World. But the Journey has changed the hero, giving him the ability to restore balance and harmony to his world. The "healing elixir" may be in the form of a great treasure, a magical object, a powerful tool, love and wisdom...or simply a fresh outlook. Thus, Lady is once again seen in the loving home of the Darling family, but now she is accompanied by a newly domesticated Tramp and a litter of adorable puppies. WALL-E, with his personality rebooted by an electronic "kiss" from EVE, joins the other robots and the humans from the *Axiom* to literally restore life to Earth.

The following chapters will explore the character archetypes and the stages of the Hero's Journey in more detail while revealing how they are presented in the Disney theme park guest experience. But first, let's explore how the Imagineers channel their creative impulses to harness the mythic energy in their subconscious minds.

Chapter 4:
Imagineer That!
Designing mythic parks

DISNEY'S IMAGINEERS CREATE THEME PARK MAGIC by combining ingenious entertainment technologies with captivating stories. Those stories contain the mythic content of the parks. They are communicated through the lands and attractions, and through all the individual components making up the guest experience including the architecture, sets and props, costumes, lighting, landscape design, special effects, and music.

Walt Disney Imagineering was established in 1952 to develop the designs for the project that would soon become Disneyland. At the time, the organization was known as "WED Enterprises," incorporating the initials of its founder, Walter Elias Disney. The name reflected the very personal nature of Walt's relationship with the group and its mission. He staffed the organization with a brain trust of his top studio writers, artists, designers, and technicians, and used the word "Imagineering" to describe their signature marriage of storytelling and technological know-how (making the name "WED" into a bit of a pun in the process).

The WED facility became Walt's favorite place to hang out. He spent endless hours there examining the renderings, models, and mock-ups, and brainstorming new ideas with the creative teams. He took a hands-on approach to the activities there, enthusiastically describing WED as "...my backyard laboratory, my workshop away from work."

After Disneyland opened its gates in 1955, the WED Imagineers continued to "plus" the park with more lands and attractions. They went on to design more theme parks, as well as water parks, resorts, retail and dining venues, cruise ships, and other leisure experiences around the world. Now known as Walt Disney Imagineering ("WDI"), the organization remains the Walt Disney Company's design, development, and master planning arm, bringing Walt's legacy of myth-making and storytelling to new generations of audiences.

In the creative process employed by WDI, every themed experience begins with a story, though the audience may not always be conscious of it. Often, it will take the form of a "backstory"—a narrative recounting a series of events that may have occurred before you even arrive in the park, land, or attraction. But while you, the guest, may not be privy to the full backstories behind, say, the Sunset Boulevard section of Disney's Hollywood Studios or the Kali River Rapids ride at Disney's Animal Kingdom, you can be sure that every one of the Imagineers who worked on them was intimately familiar with those narratives.

These and other elaborately crafted backstories serve as creative touchstones, helping to guide every aspect of the design—from the landscape plan to the graphics and signage to the color scheme and finishes to the special effects—assuring that all the elements that make up the resulting guest experience are thematically consistent and that all the Imagineers are "on the same page." Thus, even though you may not be aware of the backstory, at some level you will probably register that the experience feels somehow complete, coherent, fully integrated, and "real"...that all the many parts and pieces belong...and that they all fit together to create a seamless, holistic, immersive package.

This level of attention to the art of storytelling long predates the establishment of WED Enterprises. In fact, it is built into the Walt Disney Company's creative DNA, beginning with the studio's pioneering animated works early in the 20th century and continuing into its live action features and television productions in the decades that followed. A good part of Disney's success in these media can be attributed to the studio's technological innovations and its commitment to the highest standards in cinematic artistry. But more than anything, its accomplishments rest on Disney's mastery of storytelling and the deft and natural way in which deeply resonant mythic themes, archetypes, and images are worked into those stories.

Disneyland arose out of Walt's use of what Joseph Campbell called "creative mythology." Campbell coined the term to describe how an artist processes his or her individual life experiences to communicate a metaphor—a modern myth—that has meaning and value for contemporary audiences in the same way that the myths of ancient times spoke to people in an earlier age. For anyone familiar with Walt Disney's life story, it is easy to find examples of creative mythology throughout Disneyland— from the Marceline, Missouri streetscape of Walt's youth, idealized as Main Street, U.S.A., to the space-age wonders of Tomorrowland, which embody his enduring fascination with technology and the future.

With the opening of Disneyland, Walt's storytelling expertise became three-dimensional and immersive, engaging all of the audience's senses. And in the most popular of those theme park experiences, the stories resonate with mythic energy, often following the structure of the Campbellian Hero's Journey. In some places, the Journey may be presented in its entirety—sometimes more than once in a single land or even multiple times within a single attraction. In other experiences, you may encounter only a portion of the Journey...or the Journey may be divided up and distributed among several different attractions across one or more lands.

More than six decades after the founding of WED Enterprises, the Imagineers at WDI continue to employ creative mythology, tapping into ideas and issues that touch the lives of people everywhere. Thus, widespread contemporary interest in the health of the world's environments and the fate of its endangered species finds mythic expression throughout Disney's Animal Kingdom Park. Our preoccupation with the world of entertainment and show business is right at home in Disney's Hollywood Studios Park. And our never-ending love affair with computers and technology is celebrated in Epcot's Future World and, in countless ways behind the scenes and in glorious full view, in all the other Disney theme parks around the globe.

Another key storytelling tool utilized by the Imagineers is the "brain script." While the term itself is not commonly used by the Imagineers, brain scripting techniques are employed on a daily basis across nearly every storytelling discipline within WDI. The Austrian dramaturge Christian Mikunda defines brain scripts as "the film scripts in our minds...responsible for our interpretation of a story. They are acquired story patterns which are triggered by certain signals [that] enable us to construct a meaningful story from seemingly random information."

How does a brain script work? Let's try an example. Imagine you are approaching a suburban house late at night amidst a snowy landscape. Tiny, colorful lights line the eaves and windows. As you get closer, you notice impressions on the snow-covered roof: boot prints and hoof prints, among others. Inside the house, sooty boot prints lead from the fireplace to a gift-laden Christmas tree and then to a side table where a half-eaten cookie sits on a plate alongside a drinking glass that, until recently, contained a serving of milk. By now, you have correctly decoded this brain script as "a visit from jolly Saint Nick." You have effortlessly reconstructed the whole event, despite the fact that you did not actually witness it. The string of lights, the boot prints, the milk glass, and the other artifacts of the event were all that were necessary. Your familiarity with the Santa Claus story through your exposure to contemporary culture has allowed you to accurately connect the proverbial dots.

The same decoding process occurs throughout the Disney parks. You encounter a cast member garbed in a safari jacket and safari hat amidst a landscape of tropical foliage and you instantly understand that you are in the presence of a jungle explorer and within earshot of the Call to Adventure—or, in this case, the Call to Adventureland. Elsewhere, you come across a colorful tent structure and notice a variety of animal footprints and even whole peanut shells pressed into the walkway surface, while your ears detect the sound of calliope music drifting through the air. Evidently you have arrived in the vicinity of elephants, monkeys, and other circus animals. (Other items in the scene soon confirm that one of those elephants is the legendary Dumbo.) This place could only be Dumbo's Circus, a district of Fantasyland in the Magic Kingdom. These are just a few of the countless "random" signals that populate the Disney parks, providing you with clues that your cultural literacy allows you to decode and construct into meaningful stories.

The connections between brain scripts and mythic storytelling run deep. As Mikunda points out, "Myths are prototypical stories...[and] popular culture keeps the myths in us alive." The intersection of myths, brain scripts, and Disney's themed experiences are innumerable. The "David and Goliath" brain script (a ridiculously overmatched challenger faces off against a supremely powerful foe) provides the climaxes of attractions ranging from Fantasmic! to Under the Sea ~ Journey of The Little Mermaid. The "Final Frontier" brain script (humanity's danger-fraught conquest of the cosmos) is at the core of the storylines of attractions such as Space Mountain, Mission: SPACE, and Star Tours – The Adventures Continue. And you'll find the Cinderella brain script (Plain Jane or Regular Joe discovers her/his hidden potential) undergirding such attractions as The American Idol Experience and Test Track Presented by Chevrolet.

Today's Imagineers are well versed in Campbellian theory. On the other hand, their early predecessors, like Walt Disney himself, were not. Nevertheless, those trailblazing Imagineers managed to introduce the mythic content into their attraction designs and did so expertly. This was possible because, like all gifted storytellers, they knew how to listen to their creative impulses, allowing the ideas, archetypes, and images to bubble up, unhindered, from their subconscious minds. By tapping into their dreams in this way, they harnessed what Joseph Campbell refers to as "the poetry of myth," in which words are replaced by environments, acts, and adventures.

In the following chapters, we will explore the metaphorical Special Worlds of the Disney parks to discover how the Imagineers have translated the poetry of myth into the deeply resonant themed experiences that thrill, amaze, and delight us.

Chapter 5:
Please Stand Clear of the Doors
Threshold Crossings and Special Worlds

IN CHAPTER 3, YOU WERE INTRODUCED to the four movements of the Hero's Journey—Separation, Descent, Ordeal, and Return—and the stages of the Journey within each of those movements. Now let's visit those stages in more detail and explore how they are articulated in the Disney parks as the Call to Adventure beckons you over the First Threshold.

As with every Hero's Journey, your visit to a Disney theme park actually begins in the Ordinary World. The purpose of the Ordinary World is to provide a striking contrast with the Special World awaiting the hero beyond the First Threshold, emphasizing the sense that the hero is out of her ordinary element and that there will be changes ahead. Indeed, the Hero's Journey is a transformative one. The hero may have to develop her skills or talents, shift her outlook or assumptions, change her appearance, rethink her loyalties or alliances, or transform in other ways if she is to successfully navigate the unfamiliar landscapes she will soon encounter.

As a Disney theme park visitor, your "Ordinary World" may be the real world outside the Resort or Park gates. It may be the familiar world of home, neighborhood, friends, classmates, teammates, and colleagues…of rush-hour traffic, grocery shopping, and dentist visits…of homework, PTA meetings, and band practice…of birthday parties and holiday celebrations. Some of your "Ordinary World" experiences may be special in their own ways, but they usually occur within the context of your routine, everyday comfort zone.

Amidst the familiarity and routine of life in your Ordinary World, there is also an element of randomness.

"The 'real' world feels alive when there is a certain disorderly vigor," observes urban planner Sam Gennawey. "However, too much of this messy vitality and you will only encourage fear." Imagineering Legend John Hench once pointed out that, "Most urban environments are basically chaotic places, as [competing] architectural and graphic information scream at the citizen for attention."

Nowhere is the contrast between the "disorderly" Ordinary World and the carefully organized Special Worlds of the Disney theme parks and resorts more stark than the threshold separating Disneyland Resort from the surrounding Anaheim environs. Following the 1955 opening of Disneyland, Walt Disney lamented that his lack of financial resources at the time prevented him from buying up more land around the park site. His worst fears soon came to pass as a tangle of unsightly hotels, restaurants, souvenir shops, and assorted tourist traps immediately sprouted around the park's boundaries. It was exactly the sort of "chaotic" urban landscape described by John Hench.

Though he was probably unaware of the theory of the Campbellian Hero's Journey, as a born showman Walt instinctively recognized that Disneyland would be a place set apart from the Ordinary World, and that the park entrance would function as a First Threshold. "I don't want the public to think they are in the 'real world' when they visit Disneyland," he once said. "I want them to know they are in another world." The idea is forthrightly stated on the plaques mounted over the entry tunnels beneath Main Street Station, which read:

HERE YOU LEAVE TODAY
AND ENTER THE WORLD OF
YESTERDAY, TOMORROW, AND FANTASY.

In planning what was to become the Walt Disney World Resort, Walt was determined to control the setting as much as possible…and this time he had the financial wherewithal to purchase enough contiguous Central Florida real estate to give him what he called "the blessing of size." With some 47 square miles of land to work with (about twice the area of Manhattan Island), Walt was satisfied that "there's enough land here to hold all the ideas and plans we could possibly imagine." Over the subsequent decades, the sprawling property would become home to four theme parks, two water parks, two-dozen resort hotels, five golf courses, and an array of other entertainment and recreation experiences—all connected by a vast internal transportation network of busses, trams, watercraft, and monorails.

The expansive Walt Disney World property not only provided enough land to encompass Walt's "Vacation Kingdom"—it also allowed the Disney planners to develop a substantial buffer zone around the Resort's guest areas, separating visitors from the glare and blare of the inevitable tourist establishments that would soon materialize along its borders. At the same time, it presented the opportunity to create innumerable thresholds leading to Special Worlds within Worlds within Worlds.

In the framework of the Hero's Journey, the Call to Adventure is what gets the wheels of the story turning, propelling the plot forward and drawing the hero to the First Threshold. Often, that Call to Adventure will be disruptive in nature. It may threaten the normal order of things in the Ordinary World, making the hero's comfort zone a lot less comfortable. Or it may come in the form of an opportunity—a chance to pursue a long-sought goal or fulfill an inner desire. Whatever the circumstances, the hero can accept the Call or refuse it at her own peril. As Joseph Campbell explains, "…if a person has had the sense of the Call—the feeling that there's an adventure for him—and if he doesn't follow that, but remains in the society because it's safe and secure, then life dries up." In some cases, the Call to Adventure may prove impossible to refuse. "The fates lead him who will," wrote the Roman philosopher and dramatist Seneca, adding, "him who won't, they drag."

The Call to Adventure that brings you to the First Threshold of the Disney parks can take many forms. In today's media-saturated world, the Call may come as a TV commercial, or in the form of a print or Internet ad, or perhaps a billboard. Or the herald archetype who issues the Call may be a friend or family member. You may even issue the Call to yourself, heralding your personal desire to experience—or re-experience—the magic of the Disney theme parks.

Once you have crossed the First Threshold and have entered the Special World of the Disney property, the additional thresholds and Special Worlds within that overarching Special World can be manifold. The Disney Imagineers always strive to define these thresholds and Special Worlds so vividly that you will instantly comprehend your surroundings, understand the "rules" of your new realms, and be able to follow the course of your adventures while you become ever more emotionally engaged.

Every Disney park is a Special World in and of itself. But then each park is divided into sub-parks or themed "lands," each of which has its own threshold and represents its own Special World. Each of those lands, in turn, may contain one or more attractions or other experiences featuring their own thresholds and Special Worlds. With each new threshold crossing, you find yourself increasingly separated from the Ordinary World of your everyday life outside the park gates.

As an example of these embedded threshold crossings and Special Worlds, let's journey together from the front gate of Disney's Hollywood Studios to the distant realm of Toy Story Midway Mania!, in the Pixar Place section of the Park. Already, you've crossed at least one preliminary threshold, leaving the Ordinary World of Central Florida behind to enter the Special World of the Walt Disney World Resort (where even the name of the property communicates that it is a "World" unto itself). Then, whether you arrive by car, bus, or watercraft, your next threshold is the park's entrance complex. The Streamline Moderne structure containing the ticket booths is closely modeled after the historic Pan-Pacific Auditorium façade in Los Angeles. Combined with the epic movie soundtrack scores reverberating through the entry plaza along with other environmental cues, this evocative structure signals that you are about to enter a Special World with its irresistible Call to Adventure: "Beyond this threshold, the magic of the movies awaits!"

On the far side of this threshold, you find yourself in "The Hollywood that never was—and always will be!" Welcome to Hollywood Boulevard—this park's version of the Magic Kingdom's Main Street, U.S.A. It's an idealized rendition of Tinseltown's commercial strip—a place where movies are celebrated rather than made—and now you have an opportunity to find your bearings. As you amble down the street, you'll begin to familiarize yourself with the geography of this glitzy Special World and get to know its population of wacky Streetmosphere characters.

Hollywood, as it happens, is not just a place; it's also a type of modern myth—a source of stories that have a contemporary quality, strongly resonating with today's audiences. (We will delve into the modern myth of Hollywood, along with other modern myths such as the Old West, space exploration, and cyberspace, later in this book.) The welcome mat is out for you on Hollywood Boulevard, where the message seems to be that anyone can become a star—or at least you can shop, dine, and be entertained like one. Artifacts of the Hollywood mythos can be found everywhere along Hollywood Boulevard—from the courtyard of the Chinese Theater with its celebrity handprints and shoeprints immortalized in concrete...to the Hollywood Brown Derby restaurant, where you can dine like a celebrity.

During this stage of your Journey, you may encounter the archetype of the mentor. In the Mythic Round, the Meeting with the Mentor can occur before the Crossing of the First Threshold or after. In either case, the archetype's role is to assist you in navigating your way through the Special World. Here on Hollywood Boulevard, the mentor may be a helpful park host, a colorful Streetmosphere character, or even a printed park guidemap or the parkwide show schedule board (the latter object doubling as a herald).

Continue down the Boulevard and just beyond the Hollywood Brown Derby you'll come to your next threshold: the Production Gate, which is emblazoned with the Disney's Hollywood Studios marquee. Wait a second; did you think you were already inside Disney's Hollywood Studios? Not according to the geography of this Special World. So far, your Journey has only taken you through Hollywood's commercial district. Beyond this handsome gateway is where you'll find the world of industrial Hollywood—the places where movies are made. Like the façade of an ancient Greek temple, the gate is decorated with bas-relief images of the deities (or at least the high priests) of this society—in this case the actors, the filmmakers, and their cinematic tools-of-the-trade.

In the Special World beyond the Production Gate, you'll find the Animation Courtyard, Mickey Avenue, Pixar Place, and the Streets of America. Here, the attractions are located inside utilitarian-looking soundstages and on backlot sets. Take a stroll past the soundstages of Mickey Avenue and you'll soon arrive at another production gate—this one a scaled-down replica of the entrance to the Pixar Studios campus in Emeryville, California. Yes—it's another Special World within a Special World.

Cross this threshold and you'll arrive in Pixar Place. It's another movie production lot, but the architecture and scenery signal that you are in a different creative milieu. Here, like the Emeryville studio buildings that inspired them, the façades of the production buildings are clad in warm brick and have a friendly, inviting quality. Now you have finally reached the entrance to Toy Story Midway Mania!, with its own threshold populated by familiar playthings from the *Toy Story* movies.

Have you been counting thresholds during your Journey? Along your route, starting with the park entrance, there were at least four of them. And there is a whole other Special World with several more threshold crossings inside Toy Story Midway Mania!, which we will explore in more detail in *PART II: Mything in Action*. But first, let's merge onto the Road of Trials as you approach the Inmost Cave and prepare for your Supreme Ordeal. Sound like fun? Then let's go!

Chapter 6:
Beauty and the Belly of the Beast
The Road of Trials, Approach to the
Inmost Cave, and the Supreme Ordeal

IN EVERY HERO'S JOURNEY, the hero's adventures in the
Special World inevitably draw him to the Inmost Cave. In
the Disney parks, this "cave" may be figurative (a mist-
shrouded briar patch) or literal (a Himalayan ice cavern).
Here you may find yourself put to an extreme challenge,
coming face-to-face with marauding pirates, grim grinning
ghosts, or rampaging dinosaurs. In every case, the
Imagineers' masterful command of storytelling and
entertainment technology makes it all feel emotionally true.

As you explore the Special World beyond the First
Threshold, you are bound to encounter an assortment of
tests, allies, and enemies. This is the stage of the Journey
that Joseph Campbell described as "The Road of Trials."
And like the Special Worlds that contain them, you'll find
these trials within the Disney parks come in many shapes,
colors, sizes, and flavors; the tests may be part of the queue,
pre-show, or ride portion of the experience, or they may be
integrated into the experience of the overall themed land or
zone. Sometimes they are even forthrightly introduced into
the narrative flow, as in The Legend of Captain Jack
Sparrow show at Disney's Hollywood Studios, when the
talkative Jolly Roger skull warns you to "...prepare to be
put to the test and face the trials of a pirate's life."

The rules are different here in the Special World. You're
definitely not in Kansas anymore. On the far side of the First
Threshold, the birds sing words and the flowers croon...and
yes—elephants can fly. The challenges you'll encounter
during this stage of the Journey will serve to prepare you for

the Supreme Ordeal ahead. Your courage may be tested as you brave a jungle river populated by giant snakes, angry hippos, and fearsome headhunters. You may meet a mentor and other helpful allies—maybe even a hot crustacean band—willing to assist you on your quest, share important knowledge, or maybe just lend you a bit of encouragement and moral support. Yet there may also be enemies awaiting you—an apple-wielding hag perhaps, or maybe a Sith Lord and his army of Imperial Stormtroopers—all negative forces eager to thwart your heroic Journey at every turn.

Why must you be subjected to these tests? It's not just about preparing you for the Ordeal ahead. As Joseph Campbell once explained, "…the trials are designed to see to it that the intending hero should be really a hero. Is he really a match for the task? Can he overcome the dangers? Does he have the courage, the knowledge, the capacity, to enable him to serve?"

Often the Road of Trials will be studded with additional thresholds, each of which may contain its own set of tests. With every new challenge, the hero is forced to face his fears and insecurities. Each success, in turn, further proves his worthiness while bringing him closer to the Ordeal. In the Disney parks, of course, the tests may not be so urgent or intense. There may even be an element of interactive fun as you release your inner automotive designer to create your own virtual Chevrolet Custom Concept Vehicle, or take aim at a series of clever animated 3D targets presented by the cast of the *Toy Story* movies.

Now you reach a momentous threshold: the Approach to the Inmost Cave. Beyond this threshold awaits the most challenging and treacherous place in all of the Special World. It is an inescapable part of the Journey, as it contains something vital to the hero's quest. With so much at stake, of course, you can be sure the object of your quest will be jealously guarded.

With such an important stage of your Journey just ahead, this may be your final opportunity to prepare for whatever waits for you within. And so you may ready yourself to face the mysteries of Big Thunder Mountain by checking out the vintage gold mining equipment along with the assorted hints scattered throughout the queue pointing to an ancient curse. Or you may find yourself gearing up and battening down for your imminent whitewater rafting adventure on the turbulent Grizzly River.

At last, the threshold leading to the Inmost Cave is crossed and the Supreme Ordeal is finally upon you. This is the moment when the hero must finally confront the object of the crisis that set his Journey into motion. Here, he will tackle his greatest challenge and, in so doing, will confront his deepest fears. Often in the mythological landscapes of the Disney theme parks, the Inmost Cave will be a literal cave — a place deep within the earth. This is the lair of the legendary Yeti, as well as the sea witch Ursula, the lava monster of Tokyo DisneySea's Journey to the Center of the Earth ride, and the neon-edged semi-truck that bears down on your SimCar during your Test Track adventure.

All three stages — the Road of Trials, the Approach to the Inmost Cave, and the Supreme Ordeal — come together at Disneyland's Indiana Jones Adventure: Temple of the Forbidden Eye. Traversing the Special World of the attraction's queue, you delve deep into the bowels of the menacing temple ruins, navigating a succession of dim stone passageways and defying their ancient booby traps. Though you are in a cave-like environment, you are actually still on the Road of Trials and you'll have to wait a while longer before you'll arrive in the Inmost Cave to look your fate in the eye.

Actually, making direct eye contact with the Mara idol when you penetrate the Inmost Cave is a distinctly bad idea, and one that Indy's colleague Sallah strongly discourages as he addresses you in a grainy black-and-white pre-show safety film. The film also offers additional tidbits of background information and advice that may help you survive your adventure inside the temple—just the sort of preparation you'd expect during your Approach to the Inmost Cave.

Boarding your troop transport, you are soon on your way to face your Supreme Ordeal—a trek that leads you from the Chamber of Destiny to the Hall of Promise, then into the Tunnel of Torment and over a pool of molten lava. You'll encounter snakes, mummies, swarming bugs, a mudslide, a rat cave, a chamber rigged to shoot poison darts, and a giant rolling boulder. At times, Indiana Jones will arrive on the scene to help you out of a tight spot. But this is *your* Hero's Journey and *your* Ordeal, so for the most part you and your fellow travelers are on your own. And though you know it's all achieved through the skills of WDI's talented storytellers, artists, and engineering wizards, it often feels intensely, viscerally real. Indeed, more than once, you may feel your life and limb are actually in peril.

Joseph Campbell sometimes referred to the Inmost Cave as "the belly of the beast," explaining:

> The belly is the dark place where digestion takes place and new energy is created. [It's] a mythic theme that is practically universal, of the hero going into a fish's belly and ultimately coming out again, transformed. It's a descent into the dark. Psychologically, the whale represents the power of life locked in the unconscious.

That transformative outcome is not just the key to the Supreme Ordeal—it is the whole point of the Hero's Journey. During the Ordeal, the hero may even end up having to make the ultimate sacrifice, suffering either his own (literal or symbolic) death, or witnessing the death of a mentor or other close ally. In your Disney park adventures, this symbolic "death" may be a too-close encounter with the evil Emperor Zurg...a confrontation with a hungry Carnotaurus during a time travel adventure to the late Cretaceous...or even a narrow escape with Dory from the stomach of a humpback whale (there's that "belly of the beast" imagery again). Whatever the scenario, you'll emerge from your Supreme Ordeal a different hero in some small but significant way. Specifically, you'll be prepared to seize your Reward and embark on the often-perilous Road Back to the Ordinary World, bringing your epic Journey full circle.

Chapter 7:
Happily Ever After
Reward, the Road Back,
Resurrection, and Return

NOW THAT YOU HAVE SURVIVED your Supreme Ordeal, it is time to receive your Reward. Within the framework of the Mythic Round, this moment is often referred to as the "Seizing of the Sword," a term evoking the intense struggle that the Ordeal entails. In other cases, the Reward is described as an "Elixir"—an object or substance with miraculous healing properties that the hero will need in order to restore balance to her Ordinary World. Sometimes the Reward is earned or freely given to the hero. But often in myths the hero will be forced to take the Reward by theft, invoking the wrath of her nemesis and setting a pursuit into motion.

The Reward, whatever it may be, is a key element of the Hero's Journey. It signifies that the hero has survived a close brush with death and conquered her deepest fears. Such a momentous event deserves a celebration. For you, as a Disney theme park guest, it may come in the form of a high Space Ranger score, a VIP backstage pass to an Aerosmith concert with transportation courtesy of a "super-stretch limo," or a lavish post-briar patch musical celebration featuring a showboat crowded with singing animals.

But don't get too caught up in your revelries, for your Journey is not yet complete; there's still the matter of your return to the Ordinary World. After all, the Road Back can be a perilous one, studded with Trials and Ordeals of its own. And so you may find Randall Boggs and a team of hazmat-suited CDA commandos in hot pursuit as you race with Mike and Sulley to deliver little Boo to the closet door that leads to her bedroom a universe away. Or you may be surprised to realize that your Mars mission training exercise is far from over, even though Capcom has just congratulated you for successfully completing your X-2 flight simulation. (It turns out your Road Back to the Ordinary World of Epcot's Future World East is routed through the Advanced Training Lab that comprises the Mission: SPACE post-show, where a collection of interactive experiences will reveal whether you have truly absorbed the lessons of your Journey so far.)

One of the tests awaiting the mythic hero on the Road Back to the Ordinary World may involve a final life-or-death Ordeal. It is at this point that the transformative nature of the Hero's Journey becomes most evident. The mark of the true hero is her willingness to serve and sacrifice for the benefit of others. And so this final confrontation may result in the hero's death, either symbolic or actual, soon to be followed by her Resurrection. As author and story consultant Christopher Vogler explains, "Resurrection is the hero's final exam, her chance to show what she has learned. Heroes are totally purged by final sacrifice or deeper experience of the mysteries of life and death. Those who survive go on to close the circle of the Hero's Journey when they Return with the Elixir."

The Resurrection stage of the monomyth is a familiar one to viewers of Disney's animated features. From the studio's early classics such as *Snow White and the Seven Dwarfs*, *Pinocchio*, and *Lady and the Tramp*, to more recent classics such as *WALL-E* and *Tangled*, the hero (or characters close to them) have died onscreen, only to be revived/reborn moments later. Just as often, the final Ordeal involves the hero's figurative death and subsequent revival—a near-death experience or something more abstract such as the "death" of a preconception or a relationship or a longstanding dream or ambition. Whatever the circumstances, it's an event that sets the hero back but from which the character quickly recovers, as in the climactic scenes in *Cinderella, Aladdin,* and *Princess and the Frog.*

In the Disney theme parks, the final Ordeal and the Resurrection are typically not included in the attraction storyline. When they are, they are usually of the symbolic, non-literal, or near-death variety. Thus, after surviving the backwards plummet from the peak of Hong Kong Disneyland's Big Grizzly Mountain, you manage to narrowly avoid being blown to smithereens when a young bear detonates a cache of dynamite, launching your mine train on a wild, twisting, turning ride back to the load station. Or your near-death final Ordeal may involve a screaming, high-speed plunge aboard a possessed hotel service elevator, or a few heart-pounding moments as your X-2 spacecraft teeters at the edge of a Martian canyon.

One of the rare Disney attractions where you'll encounter a literal death experience is Mr. Toad's Wild Ride, which sends your jalopy into a head-on collision with a locomotive. Moments later, you find yourself in a comical, dark-ride vision of hell, complete with a welcoming committee of bouncing, pitchfork-wielding devils.

Disney attractions being what they are, the final threshold crossing of every Hero's Journey you take as a Disney park guest inevitably delivers you to the place where your adventure began: the Ordinary World of the surrounding themed land. Yet even though you may have been "away" for only a few minutes, you have been subtly transformed by your experiences in the Special World. You have successfully navigated your way through a strange and sometimes perilous landscape, proving your readiness for the adventure through one or more tests along the Road of Trials. You have bravely entered the Inmost Cave, endured the Supreme Ordeal, Seized the Sword, and survived a final Ordeal on the Road Back. Now, having conquered "death," you are reborn and newly purified— ready at last to re-enter the Ordinary World a changed person.

And so, when your Jungle Cruise launch delivers you back to "civilization," you return to the dock with the knowledge that you have survived an expedition into the deepest, darkest, most dangerous corners of the world's unexplored rivers. You've evaded the wrath of the Yeti, defeated the sea witch Ursula, and endured a drenching whitewater rafting ride on the turbulent Grizzly River. And now, as you prepare to exit your Doom Buggy, you find you have the ability to see the hitchhiking ghost who will follow you home. With the exhilaration of your Journey still fresh in your memory, you may look at your Ordinary World with new eyes as you eagerly seek out your next adventure.

Chapter 8:
The Character Connection
Mythic archetypes in Disney's theme parks

IN CHAPTER 2, WE TOOK AN INITIAL LOOK at the most frequent character archetypes of the Hero's Journey. We learned how the different archetypes the hero meets in the course of his Journey actually personify the different facets of his own personality. We also discovered that, whatever the stated objective of the hero's quest may be, the actual goal of the whole adventure is to see all these archetypes successfully controlled and integrated within the hero to create a complete, mature identity — a transformational achievement. And we found we could look at these archetypes as virtual "masks" worn by the different characters, and that these masks can be taken off and passed around to different characters. We even saw how several masks can be worn by a single character at different points in the story — or even simultaneously.

Now it's time to place those mythic archetypes within the context of the Disney theme parks. So let's take a quick tour through Walt's original theme park, Disneyland, and see how "The Happiest Place on Earth" is also one of the most archetypical.

Our Disneyland Journey begins as most do: at the entrance turnstiles leading to Main Street, U.S.A. Here, at the First Threshold, we encounter our initial threshold guardian: a courteous turnstile host. Earlier, we saw that the threshold guardian's role is to test the hero's worthiness and commitment to the Journey, admitting into the Special World only those who can prove themselves deserving. In this way, the threshold guardian archetype embodies the neuroses and self-doubts that threaten to hold us back as we encounter the obstacles that challenge us at key points in the

Hero's Journey of our own lives. Fortunately, this particular threshold is easy to overcome and its guardian is a warm and welcoming figure. So, assuming you have a valid park admission, you're good to go.

Now that you've crossed the First Threshold to enter Main Street Square, you'll be meeting plenty of other archetypes in short order. Listen and you may hear a herald shout "All a-*booooard!*," issuing a Call to Adventure from the platform of Main Street Station. The herald, we learned earlier, symbolizes that voice inside us that lets us know that a change is coming in our lives. In this case, the herald is inviting you to embark on a grand circle rail tour of Disneyland with stops in New Orleans Square, Mickey's Toontown, and Tomorrowland—a scenic and relaxing way to get an introductory lay of the land in this Special World— or at least its perimeter. If you were to accept this quaint Call, you would soon be greeted by another archetype: the mentor figure, in the form—or *non-form*, actually—of the folksy pre-recorded audio spiel that narrates your tour. As your mentor, the voice of the invisible conductor provides the wisdom and guidance that will enable you, the hero of this Journey, to successfully navigate the Special World of Disneyland.

Instead of riding the Disneyland Railroad, you may decide to do what many visitors do upon entering Disneyland and spend a little time exploring Main Street, U.S.A. While you're here, you're likely to meet several more heralds and mentors, distinguished by their 1900s-style costumes and cheery dispositions. They may include everyone from Guest Services hosts and balloon sellers to confectioners and old-time street performers. The prevalence of the herald and mentor archetypes speaks to the introductory nature of Main Street within the Special World of Disneyland. From here, all your other adventures begin, and it is the role of this land's denizens to help you establish your bearings and encourage you to press ahead to the other thresholds arrayed around the hub at the end of the street.

But as long as you're here, you may want to take the opportunity to visit one of Disneyland's most iconic attractions: The Disneyland Story presenting Great Moments with Mr. Lincoln. The classic Audio-Animatronic presentation has been inspiring generations of audiences since its debut at the 1964/65 New York World's Fair. And though the show has undergone a number of changes over the decades and today's Lincoln figure is far more advanced than the original prototype, the main thrust of the presentation remains essentially unchanged: you are about to be in the presence of a true American hero—and a mythic hero at that. Mr. Lincoln's heroic stature is emphasized by the stately setting, the stirring background music, and the evocative lighting and projection effects—much of which still bears Walt Disney's personal creative imprint.

The show's cinematic prologue, narrated in Abraham Lincoln's own words, provides a glance at his personal Hero's Journey rendered in broad brush-strokes while framing his Call to Adventure as a divine calling. By the time the curtain rises on the Audio-Animatronic Lincoln figure a few minutes later, you find a hero who has been to the Special World, survived its Ordeals, and absorbed its lessons. Now he has returned to the Ordinary World with the Elixir of his enlightened outlook in order to share it with us, his countrymen. In this capacity, the heroic Mr. Lincoln also wears the mask of the mentor-in-chief.

In a brief address compiled from several of his speeches, Mr. Lincoln asks, "What constitutes the bulwark of our liberty and independence?" before warning, "If destruction be our lot, we ourselves must be the authors and finishers." Within the context of the show, the statement is clearly intended to refer to the ravages of the Civil War—yet the observation is a timeless one. And as both a hero and a mentor (not to mention one of the most respected figures in American history), Mr. Lincoln brings a suitable degree of authority to his admonition. But then, as he concludes his address, he dons the mask of the herald, issuing a new Call to Adventure. For now the great man offers you the opportunity to assume the mantel of the hero for yourself as he implores the audience to, "...have faith that right makes might, and in that faith, let us, to the end, dare to do our duty as we understand it."

With the strains of "The Battle Hymn of the Republic" still resonating in your mind, you return to Main Street and make your way toward Sleeping Beauty Castle. When you reach the hub at the end of the street, take the first left and cross the threshold into the Special World known as Adventureland. This, as you'll soon discover, is a land brimming with archetypes.

Some of those archetypes have taken up residence in Tarzan's Treehouse, where Jane fills the herald role, issuing a very straightforward Call to Adventure from her open diary inviting you to "...explore our home in the trees and discover its secrets and adventures." Head a little further up into the tree and you'll hear the low, threatening growl of the story's first shadow presence: the ferocious leopard Sabor. Beware; she's still lurking here in the form of a life-size and very toothy sculpt. Within the context of the animated Disney movie—and also this attraction—Sabor doubles as a threshold guardian, requiring that you prove your courage and determination before proceeding to the next level (literally) of your Journey.

Advancing beyond this threshold, you meet Tarzan twice—first as a child with his adopted gorilla mother Kala, and later as an adult where Jane's diary describes how she became his mentor, teaching Tarzan "...what it means to be human." The diary goes on to reveal how Tarzan returned the favor, sharing Jane's mentor mask as he showed her "...the many wonders of his world as Lord of the Apes." Your Journey concludes with another Call to Adventure as the diary invites you to explore the interactive features around the Treehouse grounds, where "You may make a discovery of your own!"

Nearby, Indiana Jones Adventure is populated with its own share of archetypes—from the letters, telegrams, and newsreels in the queue that collectively serve as both herald and mentor, providing the attraction's backstory and offering clues about your adventures to come in this Special World, to the temple itself, which fulfills the roles of both threshold guardian and trickster with its secret doors and booby traps. Deep within the temple, the shadow figure is embodied by the volatile idol of the goddess Mara, while Indy himself serves as your hero surrogate.

As long as you're hunting for archetypes in Adventureland, you won't want to miss a true Disneyland classic: the Jungle Cruise—one of the park's opening-day attractions. As you leave civilization behind, your river Journey will take you into the mysterious depths of not just one jungle, but several across the globe—from South America to Africa to Asia. Though filled with beauty and wonder, the combined Special World of these jungles—filled with hostile natives, both human and animal—also presents a menacing shadow presence symbolizing the untamed recesses of your own psyche. Your skipper, meanwhile, wears multiple masks, representing the hero, mentor, herald, and droll trickster all rolled into one.

How about the Enchanted Tiki Room? Any mythic archetypes in there? Are you kidding? The joint is filled with them! Here, you are tropically serenaded by a jokey troupe of colorful birds, accompanied by singing flowers and chanting tiki idols. They provide not only a source of lighthearted entertainment, but also serve as heralds, welcoming and introducing you to their musical Special World. The four host birds—José, Michael, Pierre, and Fritz—also double as trickster archetypes, lobbing one groan-inducing pun after another into the audience. But amidst the frivolity, there's also a shadow presence, embodied by the unseen island gods who, according to Michael, "...have been angered by all the celebrating" and make their displeasure known with a violent but blessedly brief thunderstorm.

Like Adventureland, the park's other lands are also crowded with mythic archetypes. You'll find quite a few tricksters, ranging from the Haunted Mansion's hitchhiking ghosts to Peter Pan and Brer Rabbit. At the same time, Peter Pan and Brer Rabbit are also hero figures. Indeed, as we have already seen, many of Disneyland's resident characters wear the masks of multiple archetypes. You'll encounter combined herald/mentor figures in the Haunted Mansion (the Ghost Host), in Buzz Lightyear Astro Blasters (Buzz Lightyear), and in Star Tours: The Adventure Continues (Princess Leia, Admiral Ackbar, and Yoda). And the two vultures near the bottom of the final lift hill on Splash Mountain are combined heralds/threshold guardians, as is Madame Leota in the Haunted Mansion.

We will explore some of these attractions and meet their archetypes in far more detail in the case studies presented in *PART II: Mything in Action*. But next, let's take a look at how the creative minds at Walt Disney Imagineering have combined art and science to create "life out of lifelessness" through Audio-Animatronics and other ingenious entertainment technologies.

Chapter 9:
Aye, Robot
Life out of lifelessness

OVER THE CENTURIES, STORYTELLERS HAVE WOVEN countless tales inspired by the desire to create life out of lifelessness. Humanity's natural fascination with this timeless theme reflects the main reason mythological stories exist in the first place: to provide answers to fundamental questions about ourselves and the world in which we live—to explain us to ourselves. Foremost among those questions: "Where did we come from? Why are we here?" Our drive to ponder our place in the universe is one of the things that make the human race unique among all the inhabitants of our planet.

Our shared curiosity about our beginnings helps explain why virtually every culture has its own creation myth. It also feeds our apparently endless interest in a closely related theme: life out of lifelessness. In the words of legendary Disney animators Frank Thomas and Ollie Johnston: "For some presumptuous reason, man feels the need to create something of his own that appears to be living, that has an inner strength, a vitality, a separate identity—something that speaks out with authority—a creation that gives the illusion of life." Early in his career, Walt Disney himself was reportedly surprised by the emotional power of his work as he witnessed audiences weeping along with the onscreen characters during the casket scene near the end of *Snow White and the Seven Dwarfs*. To those moviegoers, the two-dimensional ink-and-paint characters had become real, living individuals able to evoke powerful emotional reactions.

As Walt and his animators realized, the art of animation is all about creating life from lifelessness. In fact, the word "animation" derives from the Latin *animare*, meaning "give breath to." According to one ancient creation myth, the first humans were molded from the earth and endowed with the breath of life by the titan Prometheus and his brother Epimetheus. Seeking to give early humans an advantage over the beasts that shared their world, Prometheus ascended to the heavens and brought back the gift of fire, enabling mankind to produce weapons, tools, warmth against the elements, and other inventions essential to the survival of the human race. (Many centuries later, in Disney's *The Jungle Book*, the power-crazed, jazz-singing orangutan King Louie clearly appreciates the value of fire as he demands that young Mowgli "Give me the power...of man's red flower...so I can be like you.")

The ancient Roman poet Ovid gave the "life out of lifelessness" theme a romantic twist as he recounted the myth of Pygmalion—a gifted sculptor who carved a statue of a maiden of such unsurpassed beauty and perfection that he fell deeply in love with it. Feeling charitable, the love goddess Venus granted Pygmalion's fondest wish and (like the Blue Fairy in Disney's *Pinocchio*), brought his creation to life. Not exactly the first Audio-Animatronic figure. But at least, according to Ovid, they lived happily ever after—a match literally made in heaven.

Things do not go quite as smoothly or happily in the various legends of the golem, a figure from Jewish folklore. Formed out of ordinary clay, the hulking humanoid golem is brought to life through the use of magical incantations and inscriptions. The most famous (or infamous) of these legends is set in 16th-century Prague, where Rabbi Judah Loew, the city's chief rabbi, is said to have animated a mighty golem to defend the residents of the Jewish ghetto from an imminent attack. However, being essentially a mindless, soulless automaton, the golem eventually runs amuck and must be "deactivated" before it turns against the community it was created to protect.

Walt Disney later picked up on the entertainment value of the theme of a hero who uses magic to bring an inanimate object to life when he first envisioned *The Sorcerer's Apprentice* as a standalone Silly Symphonies featurette in 1937. Walt soon realized his animated version of *The Sorcerer's Apprentice,* set to French composer Paul Dukas' 1897 orchestral scherzo of the same name, would make an excellent "tentpole" for a feature-length collection of musical animated shorts. Out of Walt's epiphany, his 1940 feature *Fantasia* was born with Mickey Mouse starring as the title character in *The Sorcerer's Apprentice* segment. After donning the sorcerer's hat, Mickey soon finds himself in over his head—literally—as his command of the supernatural forces he naively released proves wholly inadequate. Like Rabbi Loew's out-of-control golem, the inanimate broomstick that Mickey invests with life soon refuses to obey its master's commands, leading to near-catastrophic results.

In the decades since *Fantasia's* 1940 release, the Sorcerer Mickey character has established itself in the public psyche, becoming one of the most recognizable and popular incarnations of the Mouse. Today, Sorcerer Mickey is the hero of the Fantasmic! nighttime spectacular at several Disney theme parks. A super-sized architectural version of Mickey's pointed sorcerer's hat tops the Walt Disney Feature Animation building in Burbank, California, while even larger versions rise over the themescapes of Walt Disney Studios Park (in Disneyland Paris) and Disney's Hollywood Studios. Sorcerer Mickey even serves as the logo for Walt Disney Imagineering, neatly symbolizing what the Imagineers do every day for a living.

Also in 1940, Walt Disney released another feature destined to become an animation classic: *Pinocchio*. Like *The Sorcerer's Apprentice*, the movie centers on a magical transformation resulting in life out of lifelessness. Coincidentally perhaps, in both stories the life force is transferred into things that were once living trees but were later turned into lifeless objects: a wooden puppet in one scenario, a wooden broomstick in the other. Ultimately, both objects are reanimated by magical means.

Like Sorcerer Mickey, the character of Pinocchio soon embedded itself in the public consciousness, with the movie's most familiar song, *When You Wish Upon a Star*, becoming the official anthem of the Walt Disney Company. Visitors to Disneyland Park and Tokyo Disneyland can also relive highlights from the movie when they ride Pinocchio's Daring Journey.

The act of reanimating once-living matter is also at the core of a literary work that may very well be the world's first science fiction novel: *Frankenstein*. Despite certain obvious thematic similarities, it's unclear if the book's author, Mary Shelly, was influenced at all by the legend of the golem—or was even aware of it. But she was obviously conscious of the mythic underpinnings of her story of a misguided and ultimately disastrous attempt to create life out of lifelessness; when her novel was first published in 1818, the full title was *Frankenstein – or – The Modern Prometheus*.

There are echoes of *Frankenstein* in the premise of Disney's 2002 animated feature *Lilo and Stitch*. Developed as "Experiment 626" by a crazed extraterrestrial scientist, Stitch is "an illegal genetic experiment"—a biological weapon programmed to wreak destruction wherever it's deployed. And even though the outcome for the movie's title characters is far more positive than that of the doomed creature and its creator in *Frankenstein,* the cautionary messages are essentially the same: those who seek to create artificial life may inadvertently place themselves and their communities at terrible risk.

Some of those unintended consequences are given an immersive treatment at Stitch's Great Escape! in the Magic Kingdom. In this Tomorrowland attraction, guests are recruited as guards at the Galactic Federation Prisoner Teleport Center. When Experiment 626 is teleported into the facility and subsequently escapes, havoc ensues as Stitch effortlessly clambers about the room, mischievously taunting his guest "captors" before escaping the Teleport Center altogether.

At 39 inches in height, the title character in Stitch's Great Escape! is reported to be one of the most complex Audio-Animatronic ("AA") figures of its size. Like the attraction's other AA figures, seen in the pre-show, the Stitch figure presents an intriguing contradiction. For while the show's storyline offers a cautionary tale about the dangers of creating life out of lifelessness, the presentation's success as an entertainment experience depends in part upon the plausibly lifelike robotic figures created and programmed by the Imagineers.

The term "robot" first came into use in 1920 in a science fiction play called *R.U.R.,* written by Czech playwright Karel Čapek. The play's title stands for "Rossum's Universal Robots," with the term "robot" deriving from a Czech word meaning "slave." In the play, the robots (which are described as artificial humanoid beings composed of biological materials — more like the "replicants" in the movie *Blade Runner* than the droids of the *Star Wars* saga) rebel against their masters. Thus, once again, the hazards of creating life out of lifelessness are explored via a work of entertainment.

Walt Disney, of course, preferred to focus on the promise of robotics and the entertainment opportunities the technology could open up for his theme park ambitions. As a born showman, Walt realized that Audio-Animatronics would enable him to present a consistent, entertaining show to his audiences, day in and day out. Like Sorcerer Mickey with his enchanted broomstick, Walt's motives were largely utilitarian, with the AA technology allowing him to build his own company of synthetic actors who could always be counted upon to show up on time and deliver their lines precisely on-cue, performance after performance. Unlike Sorcerer Mickey, Walt's attempts to create life out of lifelessness—and keep it under control—were a rousing success, beginning with the singing, joking birds of Disneyland's Enchanted Tiki Room in 1963 and continuing to this day.

In some attractions, such as Stitch's Great Escape! and Star Tours: The Adventures Continue, some or all of the AA figures are meant to represent actual robots or droids. In other attractions around the various Disney theme parks, many of the AA figures are meant to represent animals, both naturalistic (Jungle Cruise, Walt Disney's Enchanted Tiki Room) and anthropomorphized (Country Bear Jamboree, Splash Mountain)...and sometimes even extinct (DINOSAUR, Ellen's Energy Adventure). Others present historical figures (The American Adventure, The Hall of Presidents, Spaceship Earth), while still others embody fantasy, adventure, and motion picture characters (Pirates of the Caribbean, Haunted Mansion, Indiana Jones Adventure: Temple of the Forbidden Eye, The Great Movie Ride).

In every case, we are fascinated by the experience of watching an AA figure offering a reasonably faithful imitation of a person or animal. There is something about knowing that a figure is artificial that intrigues us and captures our collective imagination. We are all experts at recognizing what a living creature looks like, and we love watching AA figures to see how close they come to (or how far they fall short of) the mark.

Early in the 21st century, Walt Disney Imagineering began directing considerable time and resources to an effort that would become known as the Living Character Initiative ("LCI"). Its objective: "[To] get characters and Guests together in the most natural ways possible. Make it intimate, make it amazing, and make it fun!" Over the next few years, WDI rolled out a small entourage of Audio-Animatronic characters that could physically interact, and sometimes even chat, with park guests without being tied to a stage or venue. These included Lucky, a 3,300-pound, 20-foot-long dinosaur; Muppet Mobile Lab, a remote-controlled vehicle featuring Dr. Bunsen Honeydew and his assistant, Beaker; and a life-size roll-around version of WALL-E, straight from the Disney-Pixar animated feature of the same name. Other LCI figures interact with guests as part of a larger attraction experience, directly addressing them and commenting on their attire, gestures, and other personal details. These include the Roz figure in Monsters, Inc. Mike & Sulley to the Rescue! and Mr. Potato Head in the Toy Story Midway Mania! queue.

LCI characters acquire another dimension (well, actually they *lose* a dimension) in attractions such as Turtle Talk with Crush, Monsters, Inc. Laugh Floor, and Hong Kong Disneyland's Stitch Encounter. In these interactive experiences, real-time computer animation and live digital puppetry allow onscreen animated characters to see and chat directly with guests, carrying on actual conversations in a highly lifelike manner.

Like the Audio-Animatronic figures that populate so many Disney attractions, the Living Character Initiative extends WDI's legacy of leveraging sophisticated technologies to spark your curiosity, capture your attention, engage your imagination, and leave you feeling thoroughly entertained. It all speaks to humanity's collective fascination with the "not-quite-human," which in turn reflects our preoccupation with the existential question of what makes us human in the first place. The allure of that question expresses itself in our dreams, in our stories and myths...and, as we have just seen, in some of our favorite Disney attractions.

Chapter 10:
Here be Dragons
Dinosaurs, dragons, and other things that go "RROOAAWRR!!!" in the night

HAVE YOU EVER STOPPED TO THINK about the many threatening, scary creatures that inhabit the Disney parks? If you're like most guests, when you picture "The Happiest Place on Earth" and its sister parks, you probably envision places of comfort, security, reassurance, an assortment of well-themed thrills, and plenty of wholesome fun. Yet in virtually every Disney park, you'll also find dinosaurs, dragons, or other scary creatures lurking in the shadows, ready to invade your nightmares—from the fire-breathing Maleficent dragon of Fantasmic!...to the raging Yeti of Expedition Everest.

What are these monsters doing there? Why can't the Imagineers let you enjoy your Disney theme park visit without the knowledge that you may be hunted down by the raging Carnotaurus of DINOSAUR or ambushed by The Great Movie Ride's slimy Alien? Why are these terrors in the Disney parks in the first place?

Their presence makes sense when you look at the parks as collections of mythic landscapes that serve as the settings for your personal Hero's Journey. Dinosaurs, dragons, and other monsters are very much at home in these venues. That's because violent beasts are imbued with a unique symbolic relevance that plays an important role in your Journey. As the mythologist Joseph Campbell once explained, "Psychologically, the dragon...is within you; it is your ego clamping you down." In this way, Campbell reminds us that every mythic Hero's Journey is a metaphor for the life journey that we all experience as we grow and learn and mature into responsible adults, shifting the self-centered focus of our childhood years outward to encompass the welfare of our families and the greater community around us.

Dragons—such as the fire-breathing Maleficent dragon that battles Mickey Mouse during the climax of Fantasmic!, and the captive dragon that sulks, growls, and blows smoke in La Tanière du Dragon (The Dragon's Lair) at Disneyland Paris—are familiar inhabitants within the Special World of the Hero's Journey. In her book *Star Wars: The Magic of Myth*, author Mary Henderson explains:

> In myths and fairy tales, dragons guard treasure or maidens, yet they can use neither. Symbolically, this means that they hold the riches and creativity of life in bondage, while wreaking senseless destruction. The hero's force is always equal to that of the dragon; otherwise, he would not have the power to slay the beast. But his power is of a very different sort, and his use of this force "for right, not might" is what makes him a hero.

In the Disney theme parks, whether you are the hero directly or vicariously through a surrogate (such as Sorcerer Mickey during the Fantasmic! climax), the defeat of the dragon has a special resonance. When you slay the dragon, you are metaphorically overcoming your immature "animal nature" and proving your readiness to join the company of mature, civilized adults. In the process, you are symbolically triumphing over the deep-seated personal prejudices, frustrations, inhibitions, and insecurities that hold you back from achieving your full potential. Similarly, when you control the dragon rather than slaying it, you are symbolically mastering your primitive impulses, controlling them, and integrating them into your personality to become a mature, fully rounded adult.

Though they are based on real—though extinct— creatures, dinosaurs fulfill the same mythic function as dragons when you encounter them in Disney's theme parks. Child psychiatrist Bruno Bettelheim, in his landmark book *The Uses of Enchantment*, frames the idea in Freudian terms:

> Both dangerous and helpful animals stand for our animal nature, our instinctual drives. The dangerous ones symbolize the untamed id, not yet subjected to ego and superego control, in all its dangerous energy.

The Disney dinosaurs span the spectrum when it comes to the intensity of the experience. From the safety of your seat aboard the Disneyland Railroad, the dinos of the Primeval World diorama, visible on the other side of the large plate glass windows, are more curiosities than imminent threats. Caught up in their primordial struggle for survival, they seem wholly unaware of your brief presence in their world. Neither do the prehistoric inhabitants of Ellen's Energy Adventure in Epcot's Future World. This time, you are distressingly close to the creatures (one may even drool on you as your ride vehicle glides beneath its massive head) and there is no glass wall to divide you from the action. But once again, they seem oblivious to your presence—though one or two appear ready to take an inquisitive nibble out of the Ellen DeGeneres Audio-Animatronic figure. The story is very different in DINOSAUR, as you are zapped back to the Late Cretaceous epoch and pursued by a ravenous Carnotaurus, its powerful jaws snapping just a few feet away from you as your Seeker vehicle lurches through the jungle night. (Here, and in the other Disney dino attractions, the jungle setting also carries its own mythic significance, as we will later discover.

One doesn't need to confront a fire-breathing dragon or a toothy dinosaur to grapple with the most primitive, selfish, and destructive aspects of one's own personality. Disney's parks are well-populated by a menagerie of other monsters that will happily fill the role—from the Yeti that jealously guards the Forbidden Mountain at Disney's Animal Kingdom...to its abominable West Coast cousin in the icy caves of Disneyland's Matterhorn Mountain...to the ill-tempered two-headed troll that sends you "Over the falls!" inside Epcot's Maelstrom attraction...to the giant lava monster that lunges at you deep within Tokyo DisneySea's Journey to the Center of the Earth ride. Even the heffalumps and woozles that taunt you as you ride through The Many Adventures of Winnie the Pooh end up leaving you feeling reassured (subconsciously, at least) of the supremacy of reason over blind emotion.

Some Disney monsters, however, take the archetype in a different direction, or even turn it on its head. Attend Beauty and the Beast—Live on Stage at Disney's Hollywood Studios and you'll witness the enchanted prince's selfish inner monster made external for all to see by the witch's spell. Worse yet, by succumbing to his self-centered, negative impulses, the Beast not only dehumanizes himself, but also diminishes all those around him, depriving his entire castle staff of their humanity. Ultimately, the Beast's act of self-sacrifice proves that he has fully absorbed the lessons of his relationship with Belle and has learned from her own selfless examples. Once he has demonstrated his mastery over his negative energies and successfully integrated them into his personality, he is finally free to achieve his full human potential, as are the members of his castle staff.

Meanwhile, the characters in the Monsters, Inc. attractions in The Magic Kingdom, Disney California Adventure, and Tokyo Disneyland, turn the familiar monster archetype on its head. Like the Disney-Pixar feature film that inspired them, these attractions begin with the premise that monsters are ordinary people, just like us. In their world, it is human children that are considered dangerous and frightening, to the extent that the monsters have an entire civil defense infrastructure—the CDA—in place to protect Monstropolis from being infected by any errant children that may wander across the threshold.

As with most monster myths, the object of fear in the Monster's, Inc. attractions symbolizes our immature, primitive impulses that, when left uncontrolled and incompletely integrated into our personalities, hold us back from fully achieving our adult potentials. The difference, in this case, is that those symbols of immaturity take the form of *actual children*. And yet, as Mike and Sulley soon discover, the real threats in the story come from their Monsters, Inc. colleagues, Randall Boggs and Henry J. Waternoose, whose treachery is driven by a toxic blend of ambition, greed, and desperation.

Finally, we have Epcot's Journey into Imagination with Figment and its namesake lead character. Among dragons, Figment is unique—at least when compared to the typical Western dragon. Unlike the other dragons we have seen so far in this chapter, he is more about giving and creating rather than taking and destroying. In fact, Figment is closer in temperament to the archetypal Asian dragon, which is traditionally seen as a protective and benevolent entity. Though he is motivated by the same primitive, childish impulses that swirl in everyone's subconscious mind, Figment's actions are imbued with a distinctly positive energy expressed through his spontaneous nature and his boundless sense of wonder.

Figment's joyous reaction to the world around him offers us a small revelation and an important opportunity. For while we must subdue and integrate the negative energies of our subconscious minds if we are to each form a mature, adult personality, Figment reminds us that we can also tap into and harness the positive, creative energies that co-exist below the surface. As Figment's friend Dreamfinder sang in an earlier incarnation of the attraction:

> *A dream can be*
> *A dream come true*
> *With just that spark*
> *In me and you.*

Chapter 11:
What Goes Around, Comes Around
The circles of life

FIRST-TIME VISITORS ATTEMPTING TO NAVIGATE the Disney theme parks may sometimes feel as though they are going around in circles. As is often the case, perception is reality. Many parts of the Disney parks—from the plaza hub at the end of Main Street, U.S.A., to spinning rides such as Mad Tea Party and Dumbo the Flying Elephant—are deliberately designed to move you around...and around and around. Just as often, the circles or spheres are surrounding you—from Spaceship Earth and Test Track, to Space Mountain or any CircleVision theater. And circular shapes also form the basis of many other structures and objects within the parks—including the contours of a certain very famous spokesmouse.

Once you become conscious of them, you quickly discover that circular and spherical shapes are ubiquitous throughout the Special Worlds of the Disney parks, just as they are in the Ordinary World "outside the berm." This is due partly to their aesthetic appeal: round (or rounded) shapes feel intrinsically friendly, welcoming, and familiar. Something in the primitive part of the human brain recognizes that rounded shapes are less likely to be harmful than pointy shapes (circular saw blades and cannonballs notwithstanding).

This may partly explain why Mickey Mouse immediately became so popular after he was introduced to audiences in 1928, though this aspect of Mickey's design was evidently not uppermost in his creator's mind at the time. As his own words reveal, Walt Disney's motives were far more practical. "Mickey had to be simple," he explained to biographer Bob Thomas in 1957. "We had to push out seven hundred feet of film every two weeks. His head was a circle with an oblong circle for a snout. The ears were also circles so they could be drawn the same, no matter how he turned his head."

Yet Walt's early design for Mickey did more than simplify and facilitate the animation process. All those circles also resonated with the psyches of audiences around the world. Mickey's circular composition made him appear friendly and unthreatening, and helped communicate a playful, childlike quality that today's audiences, consumers, and theme park visitors still find endearing. But there's something else going on at the same time that stirs our subconscious in special ways. Something mythic. For the circles and spheres that make Mickey Mouse and Carousel of Progress and Spaceship Earth so appealing also help us to feel connected to the universe in material, metaphysical, and metaphorical ways.

On the material level, circles exist in nature. We see them everywhere—from the ripples in a pond to the orbits of planets in a solar system. Similarly, we find spheres and spheroids in the shapes of eggs, water droplets, eyeballs, and entire planets. Exploring Epcot's Future World East, you'll discover models of some of those planets, alongside a large model of the Earth's moon, greeting you at the entrance to Mission: SPACE—a spinning attraction that sends you on a simulated journey to Mars. A more abstract representation of a planetary body towers over Future World in the form of Spaceship Earth, a 180-foot-tall "geosphere" sheathed in a matrix of silvery, geodesic tiles. The astronomical theme continues in the Magic Kingdom, where the colorful fiberglass planets and moons surrounding the ride vehicles of the Astro Orbiter attraction are designed to suggest a model of an alien solar system.

Metaphysically, humans have always used circles to illustrate our relationship with the eternal and the infinite. In Tantric Buddhism, the mandala is used in meditative and spiritual rituals as a symbolic diagram of the universe. The dualities of existence are conveyed in the Chinese yin and yang symbol, which shows the seemingly contrary forces of the universe (hot and cold, male and female, life and death, etc.) not as opposing one another but rather in a complementary relationship, each perfectly balancing the other. A similar theme can be found in the medicine wheels of some Native American cultures, representing the integration of contrasting existential forces: earth and cosmos, energy and matter, body and spirit. In other Western traditions, the circle represents a sense of the divine and is seen everywhere, from the halos in religious iconography to the stunning rose windows that adorn many Gothic cathedrals across Europe. Dating even further back in time, the circular arrangement of the Stonehenge monoliths is believed to have served a ritual function.

The metaphysical properties of the circle imagery in the Disney parks tend more toward the magical, such as the fireworks blossoming over Sleeping Beauty Castle, than the spiritual. Two notable exceptions are Madame Leota's crystal ball in the Haunted Mansion, and the China Showcase at Epcot, where a scaled-down and exquisitely detailed re-creation of the Hall of Prayer for Good Harvests from Beijing's Temple of Heaven complex serves as a pre-show to the pavilion's CircleVision movie while providing a dramatic architectural link between the earthly and celestial realms.

In addition to their material and metaphysical aspects, circles and spheres have always possessed a metaphorical dimension, symbolizing wholeness, harmony, perfection, and the cycles of life. Intangible ideas such as "time" are made material through the metaphor of a clock face, and the cyclical structure of the Hero's Journey is often diagrammed as a circle known as "the Mythic Round," with the hero's adventures beginning and ending in the Ordinary World. In the same way, the Walt Disney World Railroad conveys you on a grand circle tour of the Magic Kingdom (assuming you stay aboard for a round trip excursion) while nearly every other moving attraction in every Disney park—from the Jungle Cruise to Radiator Springs Racers—ends up depositing you at or close to the spot where your adventure began.

Mythologist Joseph Campbell described another circular metaphor in his celebrated *The Power of Myth* TV interviews with journalist Bill Moyers:

> In the Middle Ages, a favorite image that occurs in many, many contexts is the wheel of fortune. There's the hub of the wheel, and there is the revolving rim of the wheel. For example, if you are attached to the rim of the wheel of fortune, you will be either above going down or at the bottom coming up. But if you are at the hub, you are in the same place all the time....That is following your bliss.

In this context, the wheel is a metaphor for the idea of destiny. The image of the stationary hub at the center of the wheel conveys that, when we live our lives in a balanced, centered way, we can discover a degree of continuity amidst the uncertainties of existence.

Another sort of hub serves a similar function at Disneyland and in every Magic Kingdom-class park around the world. Specifically, the hub plaza in front of the castle, which forms the center of the radial or "hub-and-spoke" plan that defines the park's layout. Walt Disney personally insisted on the use of the radial plan for Disneyland based on his extensive research into urban planning principles. "Disneyland is going to be a place where you can't get lost or tired unless you want to," he commented prior to the park's 1955 opening. Walt realized that the hub-and-spoke layout—with the various lands of the park radiating out from a central, circular plaza like the spokes on a wagon wheel—would help visitors orient themselves while giving them easy access to a familiar central area from any other area within the park.

Walt Disney's Carousel of Progress, which originally debuted at the 1964/65 New York World's Fair, is another effective example of a couple of intangible ideas—the passage of time over several generations and the impact of technological change—given substance through metaphor. The rotation of the theater as it sends the audience revolving from scene to scene adds a visceral quality to the theme of progress. At the same time, the highly theatrical nature of the production, with its music and lighting cues, scrim effects, and other flourishes, combined with the lead character's folksy narration (reportedly inspired by Thornton Wilder's Pulitzer Prize-winning stage play *Our Town*), give the presentation an abstract quality. Yet the realistic props, costumes, and sets simultaneously add an element of reality. The show's Audio-Animatronic family, meanwhile, appears to be physically immune to the passage of the decades, with only their hairstyles, clothing, and speech patterns changing from scene to scene. Clearly, they are intended to serve as archetypes.

Do the mythic qualities inherent in the circular and spherical forms populating the Disney theme parks really influence how you experience them? Does it matter if TriceraTop Spin, Test Track, Aladdin's Flying Carpets, and the endless loops of Big Thunder Mountain Railroad and "it's a small world" all reverberate with the mythic energy of the cosmos? Taken individually, perhaps not. But when considered alongside the countless other mythic elements that comprise the Disney parks, these familiar yet remarkable shapes become an essential part of their Special Worlds, quietly resonating in your subconscious as you pursue your personal Hero's Journey.

Chapter 12:
Lost & Found
Mythical mazes and legendary labyrinths

WINDING YOUR WAY THROUGH THE STANDBY QUEUE of your favorite Disney attractions, images of 17th-century royal guests wandering through the labyrinth of Versailles and the myth of Theseus and the Minotaur may be the farthest things from your mind. Your *conscious* mind, at least. But below the surface, in the vast caverns of your subconscious, your brain is undergoing the same transcendent emotional processes that countless seekers—adventurers and pilgrims alike—have experienced over millennia. Like them, as you slowly traverse the switchbacks and hidden turns, each step you take brings you closer and closer to your objective…and perhaps a heightened state of mind. Along the way, you may encounter an assortment of challenges or clues that make your arrival at your destination all the more rewarding.

In the world of myths, the mazes and labyrinths that challenge the hero are more than mere obstacles; they also symbolize the complex paths that we all must traverse through our lives in order to discover our individual essential truth. Yet, though the terms "labyrinth" and "maze" are often used interchangeably in everyday English, they actually describe two similar but different structures.

Typically, a maze features a "multicursal" layout in which you are faced with multiple paths and dead-ends. Make a wrong turn and you will have to backtrack to find a different path, which may then send you into another dead-end. There's a certain level of anxiety involved as the danger of becoming lost in the depths of the maze, if only for a few moments, is all too real. To successfully navigate a maze, therefore, you will need to bring along an abundance of patience, clear thinking, determination…and maybe a map, if you have one.

There are no dead-ends or false turns in a true labyrinth. Instead, the path is typically "unicursal." Once you have entered, you only need to follow the single route, moving continuously forward through numerous convolutions, to find your way to the goal—usually situated at the heart of the labyrinth. Like a maze, though there is an overall pattern to the labyrinth, you cannot detect that pattern once you are immersed in it. And though you may experience a sense of disorientation similar to what you'd feel inside a maze, you need never fear becoming lost in a labyrinth.

That sense of isolation and disorientation is part of what makes today's labyrinth and maze experiences pleasurable for so many people. When you enter a labyrinth or maze, you are embarking on a journey of self-discovery that closely corresponds to the four movements of the Hero's Journey: Separation, Descent, Ordeal, and Return.

In an earlier time, to enter a maze was an act of courage or a rite of passage, as portrayed in the ancient Cretan myth of Theseus and the Minotaur. Theseus' adventure takes him into the depths of a diabolical maze where, through a combination of courage and cunning, he slays the monster that awaits him there, symbolically conquering his inner beast.

The initiatory aspect of the maze experience ties in directly with the Approach to the Inmost Cave stage of the Hero's Journey and serves the same psychological purpose. During the Stone Age, prehistoric youths would be sent into caves and then required to navigate the many branching tunnels, proving their worthiness in a literal "rite of passage." In these ancient cultures, to reach the womb-like innermost depths of the cave maze—a place of total darkness and disorientation—was to arrive at the center of one's soul. The initiate would ultimately emerge transformed—"reborn" and ready to take his place (with all the rights and responsibilities therein) among the world of adults.

You won't experience anything quite as transformative as you negotiate the queues and other labyrinthine spaces within the Disney parks. After all, the parks are intended to be places of entertainment and leisure, not venues for life-changing rituals. Nevertheless, there are some experiences in the parks that resonate in the same areas of your subconscious mind, though usually in a less intense way.

On a parkwide scale, the Disney Imagineers generally avoid the use of complicated layouts in favor of more intuitively navigable landscape plans. Walt Disney's original radial or "hub-and-spoke" park plan or variations thereof inform every Magic Kingdom-class park in Disney's portfolio, along with other Disney parks such as Epcot, Disney's Animal Kingdom, and Tokyo DisneySea. On the other hand, the relatively convoluted layouts of parks such as Disney's Hollywood Studios and Disney California Adventure reflect their more organic development histories as they sporadically gained new lands and attractions over the years, evolving from half-day to full-day experiences.

Zoom in to the scale of individual lands and attractions within the parks and suddenly mazes and labyrinths become a far more common sight. The attraction queues, as mentioned above, are among the more obvious examples. More and more, the standby queues are gaining interactive elements as the Imagineers strive to engage and entertain you while you wait in line. Attractions such as The Many Adventures of Winnie the Pooh, Space Mountain, Soarin', Big Thunder Mountain Railroad, and Test Track Presented by Chevrolet in recent years have been outfitted with tasks and challenges corresponding to those awaiting the mythic hero along the "Road of Trials." With their confining, dimly lit cave-like settings, some queues, including those for Under the Sea ~ Journey of the Little Mermaid and Pirates of the Caribbean, directly evoke the catacomb-like mazes of ancient initiation rituals.

In some of the parks, you can veer off the beaten path to wander the less-populated corners as you briefly lose your sense of orientation. Tom Sawyer Island in the Magic Kingdom even comes equipped with its own network of caves where the sense of isolation and disorientation can be acutely felt. Meanwhile, at Disney's Animal Kingdom, you can follow the winding Pangani Forest Exploration Trail and the Maharajah Jungle Trek, where it's easy to imagine being just one wrong turn away from becoming lost in the jungle (and possibly stalked by a tiger).

Many other Disney attractions—especially the dark rides—are labyrinthine in their design. There's a practical motivation at work here: rides that employ winding guideways or channels can be more efficiently contained within the limited confines of their show buildings. In addition, the tight turns help to isolate the different scenes from one another. At the same time, the twisting, turning routes that your ride vehicle takes through Haunted Mansion, Toy Story Midway Mania, or "it's a small world," create a disorienting effect that helps to separate you from the Ordinary World, increasing the sensation that you have crossed a threshold and are descending into the Special World of the attraction's storyline. When the ride features a spinning element such as Buzz Lightyear's Space Ranger Spin or Pooh's Hunny Hunt (in Tokyo Disneyland), the disorientation can be even more pronounced.

Then there's Alice's Curious Labyrinth at Disneyland Paris—one of only two literal mazes in the Disney theme park constellation. Inspired by such historical constructs as England's Hampton Court Maze and the (long-defunct) labyrinth of Versailles in France, Alice's Curious Labyrinth is sprinkled with characters and scenic elements from Disney's 1951 animated feature *Alice in Wonderland*. The route through this multicursal hedge maze is shaped like the body of the Cheshire Cat, and features the Queen of Heart's Castle, which provides guests with a bird's-eye view of the maze and surrounding Fantasyland area. The second literal maze—a much smaller hedge maze—fills out the park-like area at the back of Epcot's United Kingdom showcase.

Like their modern theme park counterparts, the hedge mazes of the European Enlightenment were treasured for both their leisure potential and their aesthetic beauty. Statues, topiary, fountains, and other features added charm while providing navigational landmarks. The closely manicured hedges, meanwhile, were tall enough to prevent maze-goers from peering over the top, insuring a sense of separation and disorientation.

Although the Enlightenment mazes and labyrinths, like their modern theme park descendants, were not designed to produce a real sense of peril, those who enter them still follow in the footsteps of brave Theseus. As Joseph Campbell wrote in *The Hero With A Thousand Faces*:

> ...we have not even to risk the journey alone; for the heroes of all time have gone before us; the labyrinth is thoroughly known; we have only to follow the thread of the hero-path. And where we had thought to find an abomination, we shall find a god; where we had thought to slay another, we shall slay ourselves; where we had thought to travel outward, we shall come to the center of our own existence; where we had thought to be alone, we shall be with all the world.

In this deliberately roundabout way, the time you spend winding your way through the twists and turns of your Disney theme park adventures links you to countless generations of previous adventurers around the world. Like them, by the end of your Journey, you just might end up discovering something new about yourself.

Chapter 13:
Peak Performance
Disney's mythical mountains

DISNEY'S MOUNTAINS ARE AMONG the most recognizable features of the company's theme parks, with some 18 mountains dotting the Disney themescapes worldwide as of 2013 (make that 20 if you count the mountains of Walt Disney World's two water parks). From the snowy slopes of Matterhorn Bobsleds and Expedition Everest to the sleekly futuristic spires of Space Mountain, the Disney mountains are often among the first identifiable features you can spot as you approach the parks, their peaks rising above the treetops, promising adventure and excitement.

The Disney mountains contribute an element of drama to their respective parks while also serving as distinctive icons, landmarks, and visual magnets (what Walt sometimes referred to as the "wienie" at the end of the street). On another aesthetic level, they help to soften, or even entirely conceal, the elaborate ride architectures that put the thrills into your adventure. But the Disney mountains also fulfill a mythic function. As legendary Imagineer Joe Rohde observes, "The mountain is a very, very potent mythological symbol—a symbol that, if you experience this, something will happen to you; you will change."

In saying "you will change" as a result of your mountain encounter, Rohde is describing something more sublime than your elevated pulse after braving Big Thunder Mountain Railroad, or that waterlogged feeling at the end of your Grizzly River Run adventure (although in the latter instance, you very well may have to change your clothes). Rather, Rohde is referring to the transformative nature of the Hero's Journey—the idea that, by the end of your heroic exploits, you are no longer the same person you were when you first accepted the Call to Adventure. And within the Special World of the Hero's Journey, mountains are among the most prominent symbols of altered consciousness.

It's easy to understand some of the reasons for their powerful impact once you begin to think about it. Mountains, after all, are life-giving entities. Though they are composed of dead rock, the snowmelt that flows from their upper elevations becomes streams and rivers and lakes that nourish countless plants and animals. Life out of lifelessness. Sound familiar?

Then there's the metaphysical component. To attain the summit of a mountain is to approach the vault of heaven— to feel yourself in contact with the eternal and the infinite. This was a familiar concept to the ancient Greeks, who regarded Mount Olympus, the highest peak in Greece, as the abode of the Twelve Olympians of the Hellenistic World. To the people of the Inca Empire, the mountains of the Andean range held tremendous spiritual significance and were believed to be direct portals to the gods. And in the Hindu pantheon, the entire Himalayan range is itself considered to be a deity known as *Giri-raj* (King of the Mountains,), its towering stature a compelling metaphor for the vast potential of the human soul.

The idea of the mountain as a stairway to heaven is expressed in the notion of the *axis mundi*—the world axis. As the term implies, *axis mundi* is the idea that the universe revolves around a certain spot on the earth—a place where all four points of the compass converge and an imaginary axis connects the heavens to the earth's core. The world axis, however, is not congruent with the earth's actual rotational axis (defined by the geographic north and south poles). Rather, the *axis mundi* exists on a symbolic, spiritual level and typically runs through the center of a prominent mountain—a natural place to imagine a connection between the earthly and celestial realms. Consequently, those mountains are regarded as sacred places by the people living near them, and there are many *axes mundi* around the world.

Expedition Everest – Legend of the Forbidden Mountain at Disney's Animal Kingdom is one of the few mountains on the Disney range explicitly identified as a sacred mountain. In fact, its sacred status is a major element of the attraction's storyline, in which the legendary Yeti is believed by the inhabitants of the fictitious Himalayan village of Serka Zong (in the equally fictitious kingdom of Anandapur) to be a divinely appointed guardian of the (likewise fictitious) Forbidden Mountain. Those who dare to violate the sanctity of this hallowed place will surely incur the Yeti's wrath. The storyline's spiritual foundation is communicated through various shrines and pieces of iconography situated in and around the attraction, along with a modest Yeti museum that explains the creature's cultural significance.

Like Expedition Everest, the Big Thunder Mountain storyline also treats the location as a sacred mountain. The attraction's chief designer, Imagineer Tony Baxter, based its backstory partially on the real-life Lost Dutchman Mine outside Phoenix, Arizona. According to local Native American lore, the surrounding mountains are protected by an ancient "thunder god" who will visit misfortune upon anyone who desecrates this holy place. A similar curse shrouds the fictitious Big Thunder gold mine. According to the attraction's backstory, the supernatural forces inside the mountain were unleashed in all their fury after the mining company recklessly dynamited the mountain in an effort to extract every last troy ounce of the mine's wealth. Besieged by earthquakes and floods, the mining operation ground to a permanent halt and the surrounding settlement was transformed overnight into a ghost town. Yet even today, the dusty old mine trains can still be seen racing around the mountain at breakneck speeds without an engineer or crew in sight.

The sense of wonder that mountains evoke is not reserved only for those regarded as sacred. All mountains, to one extent or another, are capable of leaving us impressed by their beauty and majesty. Even scaled-down, forced-perspective ones such as Space Mountain (its iconic form inspired in part by Japan's Mount Fuji, another sacred peak), Matterhorn Bobsleds, Tokyo DisneySea's Mount Prometheus, or the Cadillac Mountain Range of Cars Land, stir something deep inside our psyches in ways that are similar to other mythic places and objects.

What makes the Disney mountains mythic? For one thing, mountains correspond to the Inmost Cave stage of the Hero's Journey. Yes, it sounds paradoxical. After all, when you are ascending a mountain, you are about as far from being in a deep, dark cavern as you can be. However, the Inmost Cave is not a physical place; it is a condition and a state of mind. It is where the Supreme Ordeal awaits the hero as she prepares to confront her worst fears.

On the other hand, most Disney mountains come equipped with their own physical caves concealing the Supreme Ordeal. You'll confront the abominable snowman as you ride the Matterhorn Bobsleds, while the Yeti awaits you inside the icy caverns of Expedition Everest. The caves of Big Thunder Mountain feature swarming bats, an earthquake, and falling rocks. At Splash Mountain, the Inmost Cave is incongruously called "The Laughing Place" and can only be escaped by hurtling into a monstrous briar patch. And in Space Mountain, your journey takes place in the inky, star-flecked darkness of the attraction's cavernous, conical shell.

While mountains serve as a form of the Inmost Cave, they also represent the halfway point in the Hero's Journey. Once you have conquered the summit, it's all downhill from there as you commence the portion of the adventure corresponding to the Return movement of the Heroic Round. For a time you may feel a sense of exhilaration and relief, having attained the peak and survived your Supreme Ordeal. But the trek back down the mountain has its own perils. And so you may find yourself braving a gauntlet of churning whitewater rapids as you make your drenching descent from Grizzly Peak...or end up riding a wave of molten lava that sends your Journey to the Center of the Earth exploration vehicle hurtling down the slopes of an erupting Mount Prometheus.

WDI show writer Jason Surrell, in his book *The Disney Mountains – Imagineering at Its Peak*, summed it up best when he wrote: "If you're looking to challenge yourself—mind, body, and spirit—or peer into the deepest, darkest recesses of your inner self, or even search for the ever-elusive meaning of life, there's a good chance you'll do it on top of a mountain somewhere in the world." And that mountain just might happen to be inside a Disney theme park.

Chapter 14:
The Back Side of Water
Forests, jungles, and rivers

"WAVE GOODBYE TO THOSE FOLKS ON THE DOCK; they may never see you again," says your skipper, tongue planted firmly in cheek, as your Jungle Cruise launch pulls away from its berth. What is left unsaid, however, is that your joke-laden expedition into the mysterious backwaters of some of the world's most remote rainforests and tropical jungles is actually a voyage into the depths of your own subconscious mind. But the "world-famous" Jungle Cruise is only one of many journeys into the metaphorical forests, jungles, and waterways of your psyche to be found in the Disney theme parks. At the same time, they double as Special Worlds that provide the backdrops for countless Hero's Journeys.

Jungles and forests are an especially familiar sight in the Disney parks. Every Magic Kingdom-class park has its own Adventureland, promising "romance," "mystery," and "tropical rivers – silently flowing into the unknown." Large sections of Disney's Animal Kingdom, meanwhile, immerse you in the jungles and rainforests of Asia, Africa, and the tropics. You can explore Disneyland Paris' Adventure Isle with its version of the Swiss Family Treehouse...join comedienne Ellen DeGeneres and Bill Nye the Science Guy on an Energy Adventure through a dinosaur-infested primeval jungle...discover the wonders of the Hundred Acre Wood in The Many Adventures of Winnie the Pooh...and hurtle through the alien forests of the Wookiee planet Kashyyyk aboard a Starspeeder 1000 in Star Tours — The Adventures Continue.

Enter any of these environments and you will feel yourself transported to a faraway, exotic, and often dangerous world...which is pretty much the whole point. In myths and fairy tales, forests and jungles are places where sorcerers dwell, where witches cast their spells, and where there's always something magical in the air. It's no accident that Hong Kong Disneyland's Mystic Manor attraction is situated in a dense, uncharted rainforest where supernatural forces are often observed (rather than, say, in a quaint American seaside setting where you might expect to find a whimsically eclectic Victorian mansion of that sort).

A more malevolent brand of magic is on display inside the Indiana Jones Adventure attractions at Disneyland Park and Tokyo DisneySea, both of which occupy jungle settings. In the latter case, the name of the ride's host land—Lost River Delta—hints at the transformative nature of the Hero's Journey. As child psychologist Bruno Bettelheim, in his book *The Uses of Enchantment: The Meaning and Importance of Fairy Tales*, explains:

> Since ancient times the near-impenetrable forest in which we get lost has symbolized the dark, hidden, near-impenetrable world of our unconscious. If we...have entered this wilderness with an as yet undeveloped personality, when we succeed in finding our way out we shall emerge with a much more highly developed humanity.

While jungles and forests possess a mythic resonance, so do individual trees. Their scale and majesty have always excited the imagination, inspiring poems, songs, art, and stories in cultures throughout the world. In many ancient societies, trees were invested with elaborate mythologies all their own, figuring prominently in the art and legends of the ancient Egyptians and personified by the ancient Greeks as Alseids, Dryads, Hamadryads, and other arboreal nymphs. The people of India, meanwhile, had their own tree nymph: the eternally captivating Vrikshaka.

The notion of trees as vessels of spiritual and creative energy also defines the idea of the sacred grove, in which certain trees are venerated and even worshipped. The ancient Celts believed the yew tree to be a symbol of immortality, while the Druids performed many of their rituals amidst stands of oak trees. The ancient Assyrians regarded fruit trees as symbols of fertility. And in Norse mythology, the roots of the mighty tree known as Yggdrasil anchor the heavens to the underworld, serving as a sort of living *axis mundi*.

The allure of trees and our sense of connection with them may explain why every Magic Kingdom-class park features either a Swiss Family Treehouse or a Tarzan's Treehouse attraction. As a guest, your ability to ascend into the canopy of a tree and visit the living spaces of a family that has made its home there is especially resonant, merging two powerful sets of imagery: a "living" tree, with all the natural energies that it contains, and a human residence, with its created environments cleverly improvised by human hands to provide for human needs and comforts.

But the most impressive tree in the Disney themescape, naturally, is the very unnatural Tree of Life, with its great canopy of artificial leaves spreading high over Disney's Animal Kingdom. The towering icon deliberately evokes the biblical Tree of Life described in the Book of Genesis, though Chinese visitors may be reminded of their own Tree of Life, the Kien-Luen, which is said to grow upon the slope of a sacred mountain. Similarly, according to Buddhist tradition, the "Rivers of Life" are believed to flow from the four boughs of the Tree of Wisdom. In the same way, notes Imagineer Alex Wright, Disney's Tree of Life "...is the source of life and water for the [surrounding] village and Discovery Island, and presumably for the rest of Animal Kingdom as well."

Where sacred trees and forests grow, sacred waters often flow. In India, rivers have been accorded divine status since ancient times. The holy texts of many religions begin with the primordial image of formless bodies of water, and certain types of water may be revered for their healing properties, for their use in purification rituals, and as a symbol of grace. In many Asian cultures, water is considered one of the four fundamental elements of the universe, along with earth, air, and fire. Around the world, legends of a "fountain of everlasting youth" or a "spring of immortality" have sparked imaginations and are even said to have inspired the Spanish conquistador Juan Ponce de Léon to launch his famous expedition into the unexplored wilds of early-16th century Florida.

Within the Disney theme parks, rivers, lakes, ponds, moats, canals, lagoons, springs, geysers, fountains, and waterfalls are as ubiquitous as the jungles, forests, and trees. Some water-based attractions even have sacred elements built into their storylines. Your adventure aboard the Jungle Cruise includes an excursion through the dimly lit ruins of a Cambodian temple that doubles as the Inmost Cave of your Hero's Journey. At Disney's Animal Kingdom, the turbulent Kali River Rapids attraction is ominously named after a Hindu goddess who personifies nature's more destructive tendencies. Various structures along the Kali River Rapids queue and scattered around the ride course—a tiger temple, a bird shrine, a Nepalese pagoda, a trio of stone "water maidens"—also point to the river's sanctified status. First-time riders may even be moved to think of the dousing that accompanies this and other passenger-soaking attractions (such as Grizzly River Run and Splash Mountain) as a "watered-down" version of a baptism, their drenching serving as an initiation rite that qualifies them to join the ranks of other seasoned water ride enthusiasts.

Other Disney attractions submerge you in the great wide ocean, plunging you into "the Big Blue" in Finding Nemo Submarine Voyage and The Seas with Nemo and Friends. You'll explore the ocean depths with a very different Nemo on the 20,000 Leagues Under the Sea attraction at Tokyo DisneySea. Your water-borne voyage takes you around the world as you embark on "the happiest cruise that ever sailed" through "it's a small world." The Disney waterways will even transport you back in time as you tour the Rivers of America aboard a 19th century stern-wheel riverboat, or witness a scurvy band of pirates as they "pillage, plunder, rifle, and loot" an unlucky coastal village in Pirates of the Caribbean. Like Disney's theme park forests and jungles, these water-based attractions vividly remove you from the Ordinary World, resonating in your subconscious as they immerse you in the deep waters of their powerfully evocative Special Worlds.

Chapter 15:
Wild Things
The mythic world of animals

IN EVERY CULTURE, IN EVERY PART OF THE WORLD, wherever stories are told, you will find myths, fairy tales, and folk stories in which animals possess extraordinary abilities. In some stories, the animals appear as stand-ins for humans, speaking and relating to one another in the same way that we interact with each other. In other stories, the animal characters may offer aid or wisdom to the hero or may have the ability to grant wishes. And, in some cases, the animals are actually enchanted humans...or vice-versa. Examples of all these types of animal characters reside in the various Disney theme parks.

Their prevalence in the parks is not very surprising when you consider that Walt Disney was always fascinated by nature and the animal world. From its earliest years, Walt Disney Studios has populated its animated productions with animal characters—most notably the Big Cheese himself, Mickey Mouse. As Imagineer Alex Wright explains:

> Walt always felt that animals offered tremendous character studies. Animals offer a variety of personalities, either real or imagined, and provide story settings far broader than that of humans. So a vast number of characters in the Disney canon are of animal origin, as lead characters and supporting cast.

Often these animals are heavily anthropomorphized—wearing clothes, driving cars, and yes—sometimes even owning their own animal pets. In other Disney productions, the animals have been portrayed in more naturalistic ways, with Walt insisting that his animators visit zoos and wildlife parks to study live specimens up-close. At times, Walt even had live animals brought onto a studio soundstage for life drawing classes so that his animators could convincingly convey their looks, movements, and behaviors onscreen. Later, when he began making serious forays into the live-action realm, much of his effort was focused on the production of *True-Life Adventure* movies — feature-length documentaries that portrayed wild animals in their natural habitats.

Inevitably, when Walt extended his storytelling into the third dimension with the creation of Disneyland Park, he was eager to include animals in the mix. In fact, Adventureland was originally to be called "True-Life Adventureland." But when live exotic animals proved inappropriate, impractical, undependable, and too costly for attractions such as Jungle Cruise, Walt ultimately resorted to artificial creatures, leading to the birth of Audio-Animatronics.

Why was Walt so fascinated by animals? For the same reason we all are: because humans are connected to animals in deep and fundamental ways. We share the world with them and, since as far back as prehistoric times, we have lived in close contact with them. Animals are essential to our existence. They work for us as beasts of burden; some are a source of companionship; some provide nourishment by supplying us with milk or eggs, while others become food sources themselves. On a psychological level, they represent the primitive, emotion-driven aspects of our personalities — the part of us that we strive to control as civilized members of society. At the same time, animals embody our intuitive, spontaneous impulses — attributes that may be considered desirable and which we are sometimes keen to embrace.

In myths and fairy tales, animals can be helpers to the hero. In the symbolic language of these stories, the animal helpers represent the instinctual, intuitive part of the hero's personality, making the primal energies of the natural world available for the hero's use. On-screen, the Disney heroes— especially the princesses—almost always have animal sidekicks or helpers—from the woodland creatures who lead Snow White to the seven dwarfs' forest cottage, to Rapunzel's overprotective chameleon friend Pascal.

In the Disney parks, few heroes receive more representation than the title characters of *The Little Mermaid* and *Finding Nemo*, whose movies have (so far) collectively inspired fifteen attractions in eight different parks on three continents. When you go "down where it's wetter" with Ariel in the parks, you'll find her being aided by the crab Sebastian, Scuttle the seagull, and the tropical fish Flounder. Even though Ariel is half-fish herself, she still depends on the loyalty and camaraderie of her animal companions. But Ariel's nemesis, the sea witch Ursula, has her own animal accomplices in the form of the two slimy moray eels, Flotsam and Jetsam, reminding us that the powers of nature can sometimes have a negative, destructive potential.

Meanwhile, in Finding Nemo – The Musical, The Seas with Nemo & Friends, and Finding Nemo Submarine Voyage, you'll meet many of the aquatic creatures that aided Marlin in his big-screen quest to track down his missing son. (Yes, as a clownfish, Marlin is technically an animal himself. But once he begins his journey, he is essentially a fish out of water and depends on the help of the other denizens of the deep that he meets during his journey in order to successfully navigate his way through unfamiliar seascapes.) Then, when you experience Turtle Talk with Crush, you briefly become the story's hero as the show's title character interactively shares his knowledge and insights directly with you and your fellow "dudes" and "dudettes."

According to the mythologies of many Native American cultures, there was a time long ago when animals and people not only existed in close proximity with one another, but tended to morph back and forth between species. Bears were especially known for their ability to shape-shift into human form and back again. On-screen, a similar transformation is seen in such animated movies as Disney's *Brother Bear* and Disney-Pixar's *Brave*. In the theme parks, the most vivid example of this can be found in the Country Bear Jamboree show. Although the cast is superficially presented as a band of musical bears, much of the show's comedic appeal comes from the audience's recognition of how thoroughly the Audio-Animatronic performers, despite their furry appearances, embody familiar country music stereotypes with all the customary vanities and show-biz idiosyncrasies. Watching the show, it seems almost as though a cast of human performers has been unceremoniously transformed into an ursine ensemble. Yet they keep right on playing, hardly noticing or caring about the change.

In Disney's mythic universe, the barrier between human and animal sometimes seems more like a revolving door, where a dog becomes an enchanted footman and a horse turns into a coachman, a district attorney changes into a shaggy dog, naughty little boys are transformed into sad little donkeys, and a foreign prince and a working-class girl become bayou frogs. By the end of their respective movies, they all eventually return to their original forms (except for the sad little donkeys).

Of all the human-to-animal-to-human transformations in Disney's movies, the one that has arguably made the most lasting impression on audiences is the metamorphosis at the heart of *Beauty and the Beast*. The animated 1991 movie's enduring popularity has inspired two attractions and two dining venues at Walt Disney World: Enchanted Tales with Belle, a live interactive storytelling experience (at Magic Kingdom); Beauty and the Beast—Live on Stage (at Disney's Hollywood Studios); and Gaston's Tavern and Be Our Guest Restaurant (both at Magic Kingdom). Like Disney's *The Princess and the Frog*, this is not just an animal transformation story, but also belongs to a class of fairy tales known as "animal groom stories." On a psychological level, according to the noted child psychologist Bruno Bettelheim, stories in which "...the beast is a male and can be disenchanted only by the love of a female" symbolize the need for both partners to overcome their discomfort with the "animal-like" details of adult intimacy. As the song says, it's a "tale as old as time," descended from the classic Greek myths of Aphrodite and Hephaestus, Cupid and Psyche, and Hades and Persephone. Modern variations on the theme, meanwhile, are represented by works such as *The Phantom of the Opera* and *The Hunchback of Notre Dame*.

Like the Beauty and the Beast attractions, Splash Mountain draws its story and characters from myths that can be traced back to a time and place far removed from their present abodes in the Disney theme parks. The Imagineers who designed the ride based it on the 1946 Disney feature *Song of the South*. And because Disney has long withheld the film from exhibition, permanently confining it to the legendary "Disney vault" due to modern cultural sensitivities, this makes Splash Mountain, in the words of writer and podcast host Aaron Wallace, "...the world's most popular attraction based on a movie nobody has seen."

Song of the South, in turn, was based on the "Uncle Remus" stories collected and retold by the folklorist and journalist Joel Chandler Harris. Those stories were, in turn, based on ancient tales handed down to plantation slaves in the 18th and 19th centuries from their African ancestors. Brer Rabbit, in particular, turns out to be a direct descendent of Trickster Hare, a character in the folklore of the Yoruba people of Southwestern Nigeria and the bordering sections of Benin and Togo. Other cultures worldwide have their own "trickster" animals, including Trickster Coyote, Trickster Spider, and even a Trickster Tortoise.

In Disney's domain, the list of trickster characters includes Mickey himself (in his raucous early years), and also his predecessor, Oswald the Lucky Rabbit (another close relative of Trickster Hare) as well as such latter-day tricksters as Captain Jack Sparrow (a human trickster, despite his surname), who can be spotted confounding assorted "rascals, scoundrels, villains, and knaves" in the current version of the Pirates of the Caribbean rides in Disneyland Park and Magic Kingdom.

Earlier, we learned that the trickster archetype, in the psychological landscape of myths, "...represents our own impulse to resist conformity or challenge authority." That impulse explains the enduring popularity of so many trickster figures and their ability to appeal to widely divergent audiences. Even when the tricksters are (apparently) animals, as audiences we readily identify with them. Indeed, few things in life offer the vicarious pleasure of watching an endearingly mischievous character cutting a high-and-mighty antagonist down to size. Which just goes to show that, in Disney's mythic realms at least, animals are people too.

Chapter 16:
Jung at Heart
Fairy tales and the uses of enchantment

IN THE PREVIOUS CHAPTERS, we explored the mythic structure, archetypes, and themes that pervade the Disney theme parks and attractions. However, in the course of your adventures in Disney's Special Worlds, you'll occasionally come to places where old-fashioned fairy tales take the spotlight.

In many respects, myths and fairy tales share the same psychological DNA. They all bubble up from the wellsprings of our subconscious minds and therefore feature many of the same key elements. They generally follow the same structure of Separation, Descent, Ordeal, and Return, and feature a similar cast of archetypes. And, like myths, fairy tales gradually accumulated and concentrated their psychological power through the oral tradition as they were retold endlessly over many generations, continuously reconstituted through the subconscious of both the tellers and the listeners. Those stories that struck a responsive chord were more likely to be repeated. At the same time, any individual elements within those stories that found a psychological resonance were kept intact, while those that lacked the subconscious ring of truth were discarded or changed depending on the reactions of the listeners.

Yet alongside the many connections, there are also important differences between myths and fairy tales. As child psychologist Bruno Bettelheim explains in his milestone 1976 book *The Uses of Enchantment: The Meaning and Importance of Fairy Tales*, classic fairy tales are aimed more at the psychological needs of children rather than those of broader audiences. Because of the form of these stories, and because of the child's open and accepting attitude (what dramatists would call "the willing suspension of disbelief,") fairy tales come across as being inherently truthful. Even though the child is under no illusion that the events in the story really occurred, or that the characters ever truly existed, the child feels that the stories speak a higher truth, and are, in fact, talking about his or her own feelings, relationships, and circumstances. The element of consolation is especially important. "Fairy tales are loved by the child," Bettelheim writes, "...because—despite all the angry, anxious thoughts in his mind to which the fairy tale gives body and specific context—these stories always result in a happy outcome, which the child cannot imagine on his own."

Dr. Bettelheim cites the work of the Swiss psychiatrist Carl Jung, whose theories about the human "collective unconscious" and the archetypes that originate there are essential to understanding the power and timeless appeal of fairy tales. Jung goes on to argue that, "All the most powerful ideas in history go back to archetypes," including our concepts of religion, science, philosophy, and ethics. These and other ideas are the conscious expression of archetypal thoughts that originate in our unconscious minds and especially in our dreams.

After being passed down through the oral tradition over the centuries, the fairy tales that are most familiar to today's audiences were eventually committed to paper by academics, folklorists, linguists, writers, and cultural researchers such as Charles Perrault and the Brothers Grimm. Later, with the advent of modern communication and entertainment technologies, new generations of storytellers adapted those fairy tales to the latest newfangled media. Foremost among these modern storytellers was Walt Disney.

For a born showman like Walt Disney, fairy tales were an obvious source for many of his most beloved animated features, beginning with his groundbreaking first effort, *Snow White and the Seven Dwarfs*. Existing in the public domain, the stories were available for the taking, unencumbered by copyrights or licensing fees. For the same reason, Walt was at liberty to freely adapt, edit, add new characters, and generally embellish the original tales to suit the dramatic requirements of his productions and to satisfy what he (correctly, more often than not) perceived to be the tastes of his contemporary audiences. Among Walt's most significant changes: unlike the traditional fairy tales he used as his source material, the Disney versions were produced not just for the enjoyment of children, but for the entire family.

Despite the many alterations Walt and his animators introduced—often to the disapproval of purists and other critics—Disney's animated fairy tales struck a responsive chord with audiences, showing that they had preserved enough of the original stories to give the screen versions a lasting emotional impact. Even those movies not adapted from fairy tales, such as *Bambi*, *Peter Pan*, *Pinocchio*, and later *The Little Mermaid* and *The Lion King*, still contained many of the key qualities of the classic fairy tales that give them so much psychological potency, including simple plots, unambiguous heroes and villains, and clear moral lessons.

When the time came to populate Disneyland with themed attractions, Disney's growing library of animated features—especially those based on classic fairy tales— became an essential source of immersive content for Walt's original team of Imagineers. Today those environments and experiences are among the parks' most beloved. Not surprisingly, in Disneyland and all the subsequent Magic Kingdom-class parks, the Fantasyland section continues to be home to the highest concentration of fairy tale-inspired attractions and settings.

The castles, naturally, are the most identifiable icons in Disney's Magic Kingdom-class parks. They stand not just as impressive architectural landmarks and visual magnets ("wienies" in Walt-speak), but also function as major symbols of fantasy and thus as vessels of great emotional energy. As the figurative and literal centerpieces of their respective parks, the castles present a potent brain script unequivocally communicating that you are about to enter a realm of pure imagination—one that encompasses not just Fantasyland, but the *entire* theme park.

Like its counterparts in Disneyland Paris, Tokyo Disneyland, and (soon) Shanghai Disneyland, the towering design of the Magic Kingdom's Cinderella Castle allows it to double as an architectural incarnation of the mythic herald archetype. Rising majestically above all the other structures in the park, the castle is visible from afar to you and your fellow adventurers as you approach. Its regal spires beckon to you long before you have crossed into the Special World of the park, hinting at the wonders awaiting you beyond that momentous First Threshold.

Since the 2012 opening of the New Fantasyland section in Walt Disney World's Magic Kingdom, the park's skyline has been graced with two more castles: Beauty and the Beast Castle (where guests can dine in the sumptuous Be Our Guest Restaurant), and Prince Phillip's Castle (home of Under the Sea ~ Journey of the Little Mermaid and Ariel's Grotto). Though each is a storybook icon in and of itself, both castles are subordinate to the towering grandeur of Cinderella Castle. Nevertheless, they each effectively set the stage for the stories being told in and around them, conveying you to their own Special Worlds within the overarching Special Worlds of Fantasyland and the Magic Kingdom.

Along with the other highly themed buildings you'll find throughout Fantasyland, including the infamous tower from Disney's *Tangled*, the castles remind you that this land, like the other realms throughout the Magic Kingdom, is the home turf of Cinderella, Rapunzel, Belle, Ariel, and many other popular Disney characters. Those characters are the living inhabitants of the Special World of the Magic Kingdom—the resident archetypes you will meet as you progress through your in-park Hero's Journey.

As it happens, those characters may not all be friendly. Every Snow White has her Wicked Queen and for every Peter Pan you're bound to find a Captain Hook lurking nearby. Their abundance in the Disney parks and animated features reflects a major fairy tale theme. As Bruno Bettelheim points out:

> In fairy tales, evil is as omnipresent as virtue. In practically every fairy tale good and evil are given body in the form of some figures and their actions, as good and evil are omnipresent in life and the propensities for both are present in every man. It is this duality which poses the moral problem, and requires the struggle to solve it.

The struggle between good and evil is front and center in many of Disney's fairy tale attractions. You'll even find a monument to evil in the Magic Kingdom's New Fantasyland section, where you can grab a snack at an eatery named—and decorated in the style of—the villainous Gaston, passing a statue honoring the arrogant scoundrel on your way in. The conflict is likewise at the heart of your personal quest in the Sorcerers of the Magic Kingdom Interactive Trading Card Adventure as the wizard Merlin mentors you in the basics of spell casting before sending you off to locate a series of magic portals where you'll defend the Magic Kingdom from an army of Disney villains.

A similar conflict plays out on an epic scale in the Fantasmic! nighttime spectacular as Mickey Mouse battles such Disney villains as Ursula and Maleficent. As if in tribute to Carl Jung, the show's narration places all of the action within Mickey's vivid imagination, with the archetypal villains emerging directly from the mouse's darkest dreams, only to face a well-deserved, pyrotechnics-filled comeuppance.

According to Dr. Bettelheim, traditional fairy tales have the greatest impact on their intended audience—children—when they are conveyed through the medium of the spoken word. Ideally, a fairy tale should not be read from a book, but told extemporaneously, by the parent directly to the child, so that the teller can tailor it to the needs of the listener at that moment as expressed through the child's responses. This, says Bettelheim, will allow the story to fully communicate "...its consoling propensities, its symbolic meanings, and most of all, its interpersonal meanings...." If an unscripted telling is not an option, Bettelheim advises parents to read the story aloud "...with emotional involvement in the story and in the child, [and] with empathy for what the story may mean to him."

In the Magic Kingdom, the Enchanted Tales with Belle attraction appears to take Bettelheim's advice to heart. The live audience-interactive show features Belle, in person, re-telling portions of the story of *Beauty and the Beast*, accompanied by an Audio-Animatronic Lumiere figure and a cast of children (and often a few adults) recruited from the audience to role-play the story's other characters.

Nearby, meanwhile, the Many Adventures of Winnie the Pooh ride offers an example of the "read from a book" approach. The ride cleverly conveys how a child can feel immersed in a story as the ride vehicle physically transports you through the pages of an oversized book (literally a literary threshold crossing). Though the attraction is not based on a fairy tale, it shares many of the same elements—including a (not-so-scary) "evil" force represented by a nightmare scene infested with legions of mischievous heffalumps and woozles.

While traditional fairy tales are intended for the benefit of children and reflect their developing emotional needs, the Disney adaptations—both on the screen and in the theme parks—prove that these classic stories can speak to a much broader audience. Guests of all ages find that they are able to appreciate these "tales as old as time" as much for their messages of reassurance and consolation as for their entertainment value. And for those who subscribe to Jung's theory of the collective unconscious, these attractions are the closest thing you will find to a "dream come true."

Chapter 17:
To Infinity...and Beyond!
Modern myths for modern times

BECAUSE IT ADDRESSES IDEAS THAT ARE UNIVERSAL to all humans everywhere, the mythic Hero's Journey is a truly timeless story that transcends geographic and cultural boundaries. Yet some settings of the monomyth also have a distinctly contemporary quality, reflecting issues and concerns specific to today's audiences. The Disney parks practically overflow with experiences that derive their emotional power from the use of these modern myths, which helps explain why those experiences resonate so intensely and inspire so many visitors to return to the parks again and again.

But before we go any further, let's pause for a bit of clarification. When we talk about modern myths, we're not referring to "urban legends" or "urban myths" such as those infamous tales of discarded pet alligators prowling New York City's sewer system, or lurid "reports" of the mysterious chupacabra draining the blood from livestock across the Americas. Actually, modern myths are a different sort of animal entirely.

As Joseph Campbell has noted, "...myths offer life models. But the models have to be appropriate to the time in which you are living." Professor Campbell arrived at this conclusion after conducting the research that led him to develop his model of the Hero's Journey. He found that, while the monomyth has been told and retold throughout history by people all over the world, including societies that had never had contact with one another, the specifics of the story represented a nearly infinite number of variations. Those variations reflected the culture, values, period, and location of the people telling those stories. In this respect, though a myth's themes may be universal and recurrent, the context out of which a myth originates will determine the specific shape and content of that myth. This process serves to make the story relevant and psychologically resonant to the tellers and their audiences.

In the same way, modern myths speak to the requirements of people living today. While the heart and soul of the heroic quest are the same as always, the modern context endows these mythic stories with more power, immediacy, and significance to today's audiences, enabling them to activate the same emotional centers that classic myths activated in the minds of our ancestors.

One such set of modern myths that has found a home in the Disney parks (particularly the Magic Kingdom-class parks) revolves around the romance and legends of the Old West. At first glance, stories of America's frontier period may not seem precisely "modern." Yet starting in the mid-20th century (only a few decades after the period depicted in the genre), Hollywood westerns were responsible for a major portion of movie box office receipts, while TV westerns (including a few entries from the Walt Disney Studios) galloped across the primetime airwaves. The popularity of these "horse operas" reflected their ability to express the aspirations and concerns of contemporary audiences amidst the rapidly evolving social and political landscape of post-World War II America. In a world where questions of racial equality, women's rights, nuclear brinksmanship, and the "red menace" filled the daily headlines, viewers sought reassurance in the square-jawed determination of the heroic cowboys and lawmen of America's pioneering days.

In the Disney parks, the mythic vision of the American West lives on in the Frontierland sections of Disneyland and

Walt Disney World's Magic Kingdom. "It is here," Walt Disney announced on Disneyland's opening day in 1955, "that we experience the story of our country's past—the color, romance and drama of Frontier America as it developed from wilderness trails to roads, riverboats, railroads, and civilization—a tribute to the faith, courage, and ingenuity of our hearty pioneers who blazed the trails and made this progress possible." The fact that the land is also popular at the Magic Kingdom-class parks in Paris, in Tokyo (where it's called "Westernland,") and in Hong Kong (where it takes the form of the Grizzly Gulch section) testifies to the ability of this modern myth to transcend cultural and national boundaries.

Though the attraction mix varies from park to park, Disney's versions of the mythic American frontier all tend to focus on the spirits of opportunity and optimism that informed Walt's own life and career. The Wild West brain script is very much in play here, embodied by the rip-roarin' out-of-control thrills of Big Thunder Mountain Railroad and its overseas cousins. But for the most part, the emphasis is on the inroads that civilization has made into the wilderness, with the Frontierland streetscape typically featuring such civilizing influences as a music hall, a train depot, a mercantile shop, and other emblems of a cultivated community overtaking the lawlessness of a slightly earlier time. In this respect, Frontierland metaphorically reminds us of our own ability to tame our most destructive, negative impulses in order to assert our better, nobler selves—a personal transformation that's at the heart of the Hero's Journey.

The allure of Hollywood and the glitz and glamor of show business form the basis for another genre of modern myth. The theme shares several of the ideals that are bound up in the mythology of the American frontier. Though moviemaking in America was first established on the East Coast, by the early years of the 20th century the greatest part of the film industry had migrated west to sunny Southern California, with Hollywood eventually becoming its capitol. Like the Old West, the success of the industry depended on hardy pioneers who blazed new trails into unknown territories, seeking the freedom to pursue their dreams. There, they developed new technologies and new approaches to filmmaking (a substantial amount of which, at certain times in Hollywood's history, were devoted to the production of cinematic Westerns).

The art and technology of screen animation developed simultaneously with live action filmmaking, with Walt Disney and his animators on the leading edge. It wasn't long before the Disney name became synonymous with animated entertainment. In fact, the archetypal Hollywood success story of a naïve, starry-eyed youngster from the Midwest who journeys to Tinseltown—arriving virtually penniless but destined to make a big splash in show biz—matches Walt's own early biography. So it's hardly surprising that, in the Disney theme parks, much real estate is dedicated to the themes of Hollywood and moviemaking as backdrops for mythic storytelling.

Currently, those themes form the foundations of two entire Disney parks: Disney's Hollywood Studios at the Walt Disney World Resort and Walt Disney Studios Park at Disneyland Paris. Disney California Adventure, meanwhile, includes Hollywood Land, a major park zone devoted to the theme. Within their collective Special Worlds, you will find a variety of environments and attractions that immerse you in the Hollywood myth—from The Great Movie Ride and Muppet*Vision 3D to Rock 'n' Roller Coaster Starring Arrowsmith, and Lights, Motors, Action! Extreme Stunt Show.

Yet, in a way, *every* Disney theme park is a movie park, complete with sets and props, cast members, costumes, musical soundtracks, dramatic lighting, and amazing special effects. Indeed, Walt initially conceived of Disneyland as a sort of giant movie set with detailed backlot façades that fronted working retail shops, restaurants, and attractions. At the time, his Burbank production complex was regularly inundated by requests from Disney fans clamoring to tour his studio—a practical impossibility considering the sheer number of entreaties, not to mention the disruption such tours would cause. Walt's plan for Disneyland would allow those fans to immerse themselves in some of their favorite Disney movies without interfering with the studio's production operations.

Disneyland's cinematic pedigree is plain to see when you look at the composition of the park's original five lands, each of which is inspired by a different motion picture genre: Main Street, U.S.A. is a turn-of-the-20th-century period piece set in small town America; Adventureland is an adventure film complete with a jungle teaming with wild beasts; Frontierland is a rootin'-tootin' western; Fantasyland is awhirl with Disney's animated classics; and Tomorrowland presents the brave new world of science fiction flicks. Significantly, each of these movie genres is also a category of modern myth.

In its early years, the original Tomorrowland showcased the advent of the space age, which ushered in a new set of myths for the modern world. Today it continues to serve as one of Disney's most compelling expressions of the space age as a context for modern mythmaking. It also reflects Walt's personal fascination with the future of mankind and technology in general—"A vista into a world of wondrous ideas, signifying man's achievements...a step into the future, with predictions of constructive things to come."

Tomorrowland and its overseas counterparts (in Disneyland Paris it's Discoveryland, while Tokyo DisneySea has Port Discovery) focus not just on space exploration but also encompass other topics of scientific investigation, with many zooming off into out-and-out science fiction. Meanwhile, a Jules Verne-inspired "futures past" approach is embraced in Discoveryland and in the Mysterious Island section of Tokyo DisneySea. Space exploration, time travel, and other Tomorrowland themes are addressed in other parks as well, including Epcot (Mission: SPACE, Ellen's Energy Adventure), Disney's Hollywood Studios (Star Tours: The Adventures Continue), and Disney's Animal Kingdom (DINOSAUR).

But when it comes to futurism, it is the theme of space exploration that has most dominated the Disney parks— from Space Mountain to Buzz Lightyear Astro Blasters. Part of this may have to do with a yearning to push out against the proverbial "final frontier." But another aspect of the subject's appeal may be the opportunity it gives us to gain a new understanding of our own place in the universe. This notion was clearly uppermost in the mind of Joseph Campbell as he reveled in the images of the earth transmitted by the Apollo astronauts and the new perspective it inspired, writing:

> ...this earth, the one oasis in all space, an extraordinary kind of sacred grove, as it were, set apart for the rituals of life, and not simply one part or section of this earth, but the entire globe now a sanctuary, a set-apart Blessed Place. Moreover, we have all now seen for ourselves how very small is our heaven-borne earth, and how perilous our position on the surface of its whirling, luminously beautiful orb.

This, of course, is the precise image that you see when you begin the descent phase of your excursion inside Epcot's Spaceship Earth, though the current ride narration at that point focuses on how the telecommunications revolution has created "a truly global community." Which brings us to yet another modernly mythic setting: computers, cyberspace, the Internet, and the Information Superhighway.

Electronic technology was already part of the Tomorrowland mix when Walt Disney opened his Carousel of Progress attraction at Disneyland following its much-acclaimed debut at the 1964/65 New York World's Fair. In its current home in Florida's Magic Kingdom, the show's first three historical scenes revolve (literally) around the marvels of electrical lighting and household appliances. The final scene, however, presents "a great big beautiful tomorrow" centered almost exclusively on digital connectivity (circa 2000), including a virtual reality video game, computer-controlled Christmas tree lights, and a voice-activated oven. Although the show's time frame spans a full century, the Audio-Animatronic onstage family never ages a day, establishing them as truly archetypal figures.

The digital technology theme is especially at home in the Future World section of Epcot, where an ever-changing lineup of Innoventions exhibits beckon you to preview the latest wonders that the world's high-tech companies have to offer in a setting evocative of a consumer electronics expo. Inside nearby Spaceship Earth, your ride experience follows the evolution of human communication from prehistoric times to the not-too-distant future. But it is Test Track Presented by Chevrolet that truly immerses you in the digital world as you design your own Custom Concept Vehicle and then performance test it in the glowing, pulsating, cybernetic environment of the "Sim Track."

Actually, it can be argued that Walt's description of Tomorrowland as "...a step into the future, with predictions of constructive things to come" applies to every Disney theme park and, indeed, to the Disney resorts overall. Long after his passing, Walt's optimistic, visionary outlook continues to inform the company's entertainment and leisure endeavors, resulting in a wide range of futuristic yet functional technologies. Some, like the monorails and the MagicBand and smart-card admission media, are onstage, in full public view. Others, like the Disney Operational Command Center, which continuously monitors attraction and restaurant attendance in real time and then increases or decreases capacities to meet demand and prevent guest gridlock, operate quietly behind the scenes.

All these technologies contribute to Disney's modern myths, which in turn create the context that makes your theme park adventures feel meaningful and emotionally satisfying. For even though the stories being told may date back to the dawn of civilization, by reframing them as tales of the Old West or Hollywood or outer space or cyberspace, the Imagineers are able to give Disney's most popular attractions a deeply resonant sense of immediacy and relevance.

Chapter 18:
When You Wish Upon a Death Star
Disney and the mythic realms
of George Lucas

WHEN THE WALT DISNEY COMPANY purchased Lucasfilm Ltd. in late 2012 for the equivalent of $4.06 billion in cash and stock, the news amounted to a rousing herald's cry for Disney fans as well as Lucasfilm enthusiasts (many of whom belong to both camps). Here was a Call to Adventure on an epic scale, promising not just new *Star Wars* movies and television programming, but also the prospect of new attractions based on the *Star Wars* and *Indiana Jones* franchises...or possibly complete lands or maybe even entire theme parks. Whatever form the Lucasfilm-based attractions may take, they are certain to display the same potent brand of mythic storytelling for which the existing movies and attractions are renowned.

In his book *George Lucas: The Creative Impulse,* biographer Charles Champlin describes how Lucas deliberately viewed his *Star Wars* saga through a mythological lens.

> From early folklore writings from many different cultures, Lucas devoured the great themes: epic struggles between good and evil, heroes and villains, magical princes and ogres, heroines and evil princesses, the transmission from fathers to sons of the powers of both good and evil. What the myths revealed to Lucas, among other things, was the capacity of the human imagination to conceive alternate realities to cope with reality: figures and places and events that were before now or beyond now but were rich with meaning to our present.

By expertly blending the universal archetypes and structure of the classic Hero's Journey with themes and ideas that are relevant to contemporary audiences, Lucas was able to craft a high-tech modern myth that continues to resonate on every entertainment platform—from motion pictures and television shows to video games and theme park experiences.

The very first words in every episode of the cinematic *Star Wars* saga establish the stories' context: *"A long time ago in a galaxy far, far away..."* With these words, Lucas places the saga solidly in the realm of fairy tales. Indeed, many of the elements in *Star Wars* are familiar to readers of fairy tales, including knights, princesses, wizards, monsters, and deep, impenetrable forests populated by helpful woodland critters. But with the mention of a distant galaxy, Lucas also hints that *Star Wars* may really be a science fiction epic. That implication is borne out as the stories unfold, with their starships, extraterrestrials, energy weapons, droids, and cyborgs.

It turns out that *Star Wars* draws its mythic power from both storytelling genres—science fiction and fairy tales. Combined, they allow the saga to resonate on many levels while supporting the stories' core mythic idea. As mythologist Joseph Campbell explained to journalist Bill Moyers:

> [*Star Wars*] shows the state as a machine and asks, "Is the machine going to crush humanity or serve humanity?" Humanity comes not from the machine but from the heart... Now, when Luke Skywalker unmasks his father [at the end of *Episode VI: Return of the Jedi*] he is taking off the machine role that the father has played. The father was the uniform. That is power, the state role.

Like *Star Wars*, the four feature films of the *Indiana Jones* series are also invested with mythic energy, but they approach the Hero's Journey from the context of a very different time and place. Instead of being set *"A long time ago, in a galaxy far, far away...,"* Indy's daredevil adventures take place in the relatively recent past, in various locales here on our own world that are sometimes remote and exotic, and often dangerous, but still reasonably accessible.

A large part of Indy's appeal may be attributed to his basic humanity. Though he's usually in superb physical condition, Indy is in no way a superhero. He is vulnerable to injury and pain, can sometimes be shortsighted and obstinate, and must occasionally wrestle with moral dilemmas. In these respects, Indy follows closely in the footsteps of a long line of mythic heroes whose human fallibilities are countered by their skills, resourcefulness, courage, determination, and sense of duty—from Jason and his loyal Argonauts to Beowulf to Robin Hood.

Adding to the mythic aura of the movies is the occult nature of Indy's quests. They inevitably center on the acquisition of objects with supernatural properties such as the Ark of the Covenant, the three sacred Sankara stones, the Holy Grail, an extraterrestrial crystal skull, and assorted other mystical relics. But even though his quests, initially, may be selfishly motivated (not in a financial sense, perhaps, but rather to satisfy his lust for beating the odds and recovering artifacts that have eluded lesser archaeologists), Indy inevitably ends up putting his life on the line in order to rescue others from imminent doom— sometimes sacrificing his precious archaeological prizes in the process.

Ever since Disney announced its purchase of Lucasfilm, speculation has swirled around the question of how the Disney Imagineers might integrate the *Star Wars* and *Indiana Jones* franchises into the parks over the next few years. As of this book's publication date, their plans remain tightly under wraps. But we may be able to gain a few insights by looking at what Disney and Lucasfilm have produced together prior to the acquisition.

As it happens, the first Disney-Lucas collaboration revolved around neither *Star Wars* nor *Indiana Jones*...or any other existing movie franchise for that matter. *Captain EO*, a 3D science fiction film starring Michael Jackson, directed by Francis Ford Coppola, and executive produced by George Lucas, was exhibited at Epcot and Disneyland Park beginning in 1986. It was later added to the attraction lineup of Disneyland Park in Paris and Tokyo Disneyland. After being retired in the mid-1990s, the show was revived in 2010 following Jackson's untimely death.

Though *Captain EO* is a standalone production, unconnected with any of the Lucasfilm franchises, its mythic themes (along with its production design) are highly derivative of the *Star Wars* movies. Both the *Star Wars* saga and *Captain EO* are, at their heart, stories of transformation and redemption. For *Captain EO*'s titular hero, the power of music is his Force, capable of causing profound changes in everything and everyone within earshot.

In mythological terms, music (like the Force) can be seen as a metaphor representing the civilizing potential of our higher selves that allows us to transcend our more destructive, negative impulses. In *Captain EO*, the ability to make music seems to be the sole competency of EO and his bumbling spaceship crew. Yet it is enough to transform EO and his "loser" crew into a team of interplanetary heroes. In the process, the movie's threatening, spider-like Supreme Leader (played by Angelica Huston) morphs into a kindhearted and radiantly beautiful maiden, her zombie-like henchmen and robot warriors are turned into sequined dancers, and her rotting, trash-strewn planet becomes an Arcadian paradise of stately Greek temples.

The Disney-Lucasfilm partnership behind *Captain EO* continued with the creation of the original Star Tours attraction, which opened at Disneyland Park in 1987 and later at Disney's parks in Tokyo, Orlando, and Paris. The attraction completely immersed guests in the *Star Wars* universe, with art direction, sound effects, lighting, music, character design, and other elements closely modeled on those of the movies.

Set in a period soon after the events in *Episode VI: Return of the Jedi*, the attraction brought familiar *Star Wars* characters (R2-D2, C-3PO) together with new characters (a couple of garrulous G2 "goose" droids, a fledgling RX-24 pilot droid). Familiar spacecraft (the *Death Star*, an Imperial Star Destroyer, assorted X-wing and TIE fighters) were featured alongside new ones (a StarSpeeder 3000, the Star Tours orbital spaceport), and familiar situations (an encounter with a Star Destroyer's tractor beam, a space dogfight over the *Death Star*) were juxtaposed with new predicaments (a narrow escape from a comet swarm, a near-collision with a fuel truck). Yet curiously, the attraction was devoid of any reference to the Force. On the other hand, like the *Star Wars* movies, the power of mythic storytelling was strong in Star Tours, and it featured all four of the key movements of the Hero's Journey— Separation, Descent, Ordeal, and Return—along with several of the stages within those movements.

The same mythic energy is on display in the attraction's successor, Star Tours: The Adventures Continue, which debuted at Disney's Hollywood Studios and Disneyland Park in 2011 and two years later at Tokyo Disneyland. The title is misleading, as it conveys that the attraction is a sequel to the original Star Tours when, in fact, it is actually a prequel, set between the events in *Episode III: Revenge of the Sith* and *Episode IV: A New Hope*. Nevertheless, like its predecessor, an aura of mythic storytelling surrounds the attraction, penetrates it, and binds all its many varied elements together. And once again, new elements unique to the attraction are juxtaposed with characters, locations, and situations familiar to fans of the saga.

Both attractions are propelled by the same mythic thrust as the movies. In both cases, the droid pilots (and, by extension, the passengers) accept the Call to Adventure, ultimately undergoing near-death experiences to complete important missions. In the original Star Tours, the impromptu mission (destroy the new *Death Star*) is presumably vital to the survival of the newly reconstructed Galactic Republic. In Star Tours: The Adventures Continue, the story revolves around a quest to deliver a "rebel spy" (identified as one of the passengers aboard the StarSpeeder) to a safe haven somewhere in the galaxy—a task that could prove essential to the success of the besieged Rebel Alliance. Updated show technology enables the attraction to cycle through 54 different story variations, all of which follow the framework of the Hero's Journey.

The variability of the updated Star Tours experience, along with its element of personalization (at least for the one passenger on each ride singled out as the "rebel spy") lends the attraction a sense of unpredictability and spontaneity. After all, you never know which combination of scenes you're going to get on any given "voyage."

The elements of unpredictability and spontaneity are more authentic for audiences of the Jedi Training Academy—but especially for the sixteen or so children selected from the spectators to be "Jedi Younglings" and taken under the tutelage of a Jedi Master. Garbed in Jedi robes and armed with training lightsabers, the Younglings are mentored in the ways of the Force. Their brief training is then put to the test by the sudden appearance of Darth

Vader, Darth Maul, and a pair of Imperial stormtroopers. Together, the Younglings must gather their courage and fight off the Dark Side. When they ultimately succeed, they are ceremoniously promoted to the status of "Padawan."

The live interactive show, presented at Disneyland Park and Disney's Hollywood Studios, carries forward the transformational theme that runs through all the *Star Wars* stories. But there is another major *Star Wars* theme that shares the spotlight in Jedi Training Academy: the mythic role of the mentor. The mentor, of course, is only one of many archetypes found in the Hero's Journey. But it is an archetype that is central to every movie in the *Star Wars* saga.

In an important respect, *Star Wars* is really a story about the rewards and perils of being a mentor. Every episode spends considerable screen time focusing on the pairings of mentors and their pupils, beginning (in *Episode I*) with Qui-Gon and Obi-Wan, and Darth Sidious (AKA Senator Palpatine) and Darth Maul. By *Episode VI*, we find Darth Sidious (now Emperor Palpatine) paired with Darth Vader, while Yoda has been mentoring Vader's son, Luke Skywalker.

George Lucas' preoccupation with the mentor-pupil relationship may have been shaped by his own rewarding experiences with mentors early in his cinema career—most famously under the wing of director Francis Ford Coppola, with whom he would later become a creative collaborator. Whatever the case, as a live interactive experience, Jedi Training Academy currently stands as one of the most personalized, immersive experiences in the Lucasfilm-Disney collection.

Attractions inspired by the *Indiana Jones* franchise are nearly as prevalent in the Disney parks as those based on *Star Wars*. At Disney's Hollywood Studios, Indy has a conspicuous presence in two different attractions. He appears in Animatronic form in The Great Movie ride with his fellow adventurer Sallah as they retrieve the Ark of the Covenant from the Well of Souls in a brief but highly detailed re-creation of a scene from *Raiders of the Lost Ark*. Nearby, in the Indiana Jones Stunt Spectacular! show, Indy is played by a stuntman who re-enacts several breathtaking stunts from the same movie, accompanied by a stunt double for Marion Ravenwood.

Both attractions debuted with the opening of the park (then known as Disney-MGM Studios Theme Park) in 1989 and both attractions continue today, having absorbed only minor changes over the years. The slow pace of the ride vehicle in The Great Movie Ride, combined with the close proximity of the Animatronic characters, gives audiences the opportunity to better appreciate the meticulous work that went into the Well of Souls scene. The overall effect is highly immersive, and the atmosphere of mystery and foreboding is almost palpable. But it is the stunt show that best captures the giddy excitement of the Indiana Jones movies, thanks to the enthusiastic efforts of the live cast and crew and the inclusion of several impressive action sequences. At the show's climax, you can even feel the heat of the explosions on your face.

While both of these attractions expertly capture the look and feel of the Indy films, they are really more about the modern myth of Hollywood moviemaking. To find a Disney attraction that will truly immerse you in the mythic world of the *Indiana Jones* franchise, you must travel to Paris or Anaheim or Tokyo (assuming you are not already in one of those locations, that is).

When Indiana Jones et le Temple du Péril opened at Disneyland Paris in 1993, it became the first Disney thrill ride based on the Indy franchise. The setting, an abandoned archaeological camp where a previous party of explorers reportedly vanished without a trace, feels like it's straight out of an Indiana Jones movie—specifically *Indiana Jones and the Temple of Doom*—thanks to the mine car-style roller coaster vehicles and the pseudo-Indian stone architecture. The only thing that's missing is Indiana Jones himself. In fact, Temple du Péril is the only Indy attraction in which the title character is utterly absent. This, however, in no way diminishes the wonderfully ominous mood of the queue as you approach the mythic Inmost Cave, and the adrenaline rush you feel as you challenge the Supreme Ordeal of the ride itself.

Indy is very much present in the flesh (or whatever passes for "flesh" in the world of Audio-Animatronic figures) at Indiana Jones Adventure: Temple of the Forbidden Eye in Disneyland Park (opened in 1995) and Indiana Jones Adventure: Temple of the Crystal Skull in Tokyo DisneySea (opened in 2001). He appears at key moments in both experiences, which feature all the movements and stages of the Hero's Journey—especially the Descent and Ordeal movements. The two attractions are very similar, combining the most exciting features of a dark ride, motion base simulator, and roller coaster. And, like Star Tours: The Adventures Continue, both Indy attractions reportedly contain randomized variable elements, with as many as 160,000 different combinations of sound, motions, and show action cues making it extremely unlikely that you will ever have the same experience twice, no matter how often you may ride.

What does the current Disney-Lucasfilm track record tell us about the possible direction of future attractions based on the *Star Wars* and *Indiana Jones* franchises? In looking at the existing attractions, it's significant that they all faithfully sustain George Lucas' passion for mythic storytelling. So it's probably safe to assume that any new Indy or Star Wars-themed attractions, zones, or parks will continue that approach.

Also, as we have seen, all but a few of the current attractions expand the Star Wars and Indy universes, adding new characters, vehicles, settings, and scenarios to the mix rather than merely replicating what has been established on-screen. But among the elements that have carried through from the movies are an emphasis on big themes such as humanity versus soulless technology, good versus evil, and the potential for ordinary people to do heroic things. As this has been a successful formula thus far, it's a good bet that we'll see a continuation of both these trends—expanded universes and big themes—in the attractions to come.

Ironically, while the theme of humanity versus the machine is a major part of the Star Wars mythos, the Star Tours and Indiana Jones Adventure attractions are noteworthy for their artful use of advanced and even revolutionary entertainment technologies. But on closer inspection, that's not ironic at all. In the *Star Wars* movies, Luke, Han, Leia, and all the other members of the Rebel Alliance also utilize advanced technology to achieve their goals. But, unlike those working for the Galactic Empire, the Rebels enlist their technology for the sake of freedom rather than to perpetuate the requirements of a mechanized authoritarian state. Similarly, while the Disney Imagineers often incorporate advanced ride and show technologies into their attractions, it is always done in the service of storytelling, and never the other way around. This is yet another trend we can expect to see continued as new Star Wars and/or Indy-themed attractions, zones, or parks come online.

Finally, as entertainment technologies continue to advance, it's likely that the Imagineers will find ways to allow greater degrees of individual guest interaction. The newest generation of Star Wars and/or Indy-themed attractions will almost certainly offer more personalized and immersive experiences than anything that's been done before. Which means, more than ever, Disney will be able to assure that "every guest is a hero."

PART II
MYTHING IN ACTION
Attraction Case Studies

MYTHING IN ACTION
Introduction

IN PART I OF THIS BOOK, we examined Joseph Campbell's theory of the Hero's Journey and explored how mythic storytelling plays a major role in your experience of the Disney theme parks. Now, in Part II, we will analyze scene-by-scene how these mythic elements come together in ten individual attractions.

As we've previously determined, the Hero's Journey is omnipresent in the Disney parks. It can be found in virtually every attraction to one degree or another. Some attractions propel you through the entire Journey, while others feature only a portion of the Journey. For this section, I have selected ten attractions in which the Hero's Journey is most fully realized. Some are classic attractions, while others are more recent. Where somewhat different versions of the attraction exist in different parks (such as Pirates of the Caribbean and Twilight Zone Tower of Terror), for simplicity's sake I have opted to confine the analysis to only one version.

Of course there are a lot more attractions worthy of mythic analysis than can be contained in this book. However, those attractions will have to wait for future volumes in the *Every Guest is a Hero* collection. For now, the following case studies should provide a helpful introduction to the recreational sport of myth-spotting...and perhaps inspire you to embark on your own myth-spotting adventure the next time you're visiting one of the Disney theme parks.

Just Going for a Spin
Mission: SPACE

WITH THE 2003 OPENING OF MISSION: SPACE AT EPCOT, Walt
Disney Imagineering introduced a space-themed attraction
that surpassed any that had ever been attempted before—
conceptually, technologically, and experientially. The show
premise transports you to the year 2036, a time when
humanity's drive to explore outer space is enjoying a
renaissance. Responding to the burgeoning demand for new
astronauts, the spacefaring nations of the world have combined their technological and human resources to establish
the ISTC—the International Space Training Center—to
recruit and prepare a new generation of astronauts to
explore the far reaches of our solar system. As luck would
have it, the ISTC installation here at Epcot is currently
seeking astronaut trainees to undertake the agency's most
ambitious adventure yet: the exploration of the planet Mars.
And since you seem to be interested, you are invited to
apply within to see if you qualify.

The experience, like most Hero's Journeys, begins in the
Ordinary World. In this case, it's the optimistically forward-
looking setting of Epcot's Future World East, where the
focus is on natural sciences and industrial technology—
friendly territory for enterprises devoted to exploration and
technological innovation.

The first of your many Calls to Adventure is issued by
the building's alluring exterior architecture, with its
swooping lines echoing the orbital trajectory graphs you
will see again and again during your experience inside.
Drawing closer, you soon arrive in an outdoor area the
Imagineers have dubbed "Planetary Plaza," where
sculptural spheres representing Earth, the moon, Jupiter and
Mars announce the space exploration theme.

The Earth sphere doubles as the Mission: SPACE marquee, with the name of the attraction riding the stylized exhaust plume of a scale model of the X-2 space vehicle. This is your first glimpse of the voyage awaiting you — a herald moment and one of several reiterations of the Call to Adventure. The moon sphere, meanwhile, features 30 markers commemorating every lunar mission, both manned and robotic, between 1959 and 1976. These and other tributes to the history of space exploration are there to remind you that a hero does not undertake the quest lightly. If you accept your Call to Adventure, you will be expected to shoulder the burden of that history while carrying forward mankind's hopes and dreams for a future beyond our home planet.

Entering the ISTC, you cross the first threshold into the Special World of the astronaut recruit. As you do so, you may notice the ISTC motto emblazoned on the circular wall: "We choose to go!" The motto is also incorporated into the Mission: SPACE logo and is taken from a line in a 1962 speech by President John F. Kennedy:

> We choose to go to the moon in this decade and do the other things, not because they are easy, but because they are hard, because that goal will serve to organize and measure the best of our energies and skills, because that challenge is one that we are willing to accept, one we are unwilling to postpone, and one which we intend to win, and the others, too.

Besides its inspirational qualities, this statement perfectly encapsulates (no pun intended) the spirit of service and sacrifice that defines the hero archetype.

Throughout your queue and pre-show experiences, you are repeatedly alerted via signage, videos, and live threshold guardians (the attraction hosts) to the intense nature of the experience ahead.[3] A full-size mock-up of the ride vehicle positioned near the entrance provides an especially vivid preview of the confining nature of the ride environment. While they serve the practical purpose of winnowing out Guests who shouldn't ride this attraction for physical or other reasons, the repeated advisories also perform the mythic function of admitting only those who believe they are ready to meet the challenges of the adventure ahead and are prepared to serve and sacrifice. In other words: true heroes.

Having crossed the first threshold, you find yourself in the Space Simulation Lab. In typically mythic fashion, it is here that you begin to comprehend the "lay of the land" — the rules and conditions of this Special World. In addition to the mock-up of the X-2 Flight Trainer, you'll see a large backlit graphic of the (fictional) Mars-bound X-2 Deep Space Shuttle. There's also a scale model of the (equally fictional) X-1 spacecraft (the X-2's predecessor) suspended overhead, along with a full-scale Apollo-era Lunar Roving Vehicle display unit built by NASA and on loan from the Smithsonian Institution's National Air and Space Museum. But perhaps the most impressive item in the Space Simulation Lab is the 35-foot-tall rotating Gravity Wheel — a feature of the X-1 spacecraft.

The X-1 spacecraft model, the Gravity Wheel, and the Apollo Lunar Roving Vehicle reinforce the "space center" brain script. At the same time, they add a sense of history to the ISTC, presenting your imminent training exercise as the continuation of an ongoing legacy of human space

---

[3] Early in the queue, you are given the opportunity to join either the Orange Team (for the full experience) or the Green Team (for a "less intense" version of the ride). For the purposes of this case study, you will experience the attraction as a member of the Orange Team.

exploration. Within the attraction storyline, those items embody the past; you and your fellow astronaut recruits, meanwhile, represent the future. Like the Planetary Plaza markers and inscriptions, such artifacts remind you that heroes are often required to accept the torch from their predecessors and carry it onward.

The next threshold crossing brings you to the Training Operations Room—the equivalent of a Mission Control center for earthbound flight training sessions. Here, several large monitors display "live" video feeds of astronaut training activities taking place at this facility and at other ISTC locations around the world. By entering this room, you have moved deeper into the Special World of the ISTC, beginning your Approach to the Inmost Cave where your Supreme Ordeal awaits. And with each new stage of your Journey, you are arming yourself with helpful knowledge. At the same time, seeing the activities at the "other" ISTC locales reinforces the idea that you are taking part in a shared adventure—that there are other aspiring heroes like yourself striving to move the mission forward.

From here, your next stop is Team Dispatch, where an ISTC "dispatch officer" (another threshold guardian/attraction host) organizes you and your fellow astronaut candidates into teams of four and sends you to the Ready Room for the first of several preparatory briefings.

In the Ready Room, you finally meet your mentor—an ISTC official who introduces himself as "Capcom" (the facility's "capsule communicator"—the only person in Mission Control permitted to talk directly with the astronauts during a space mission). Addressing you via a video screen mounted above a row of spacesuit lockers, Capcom issues your formal Call to Adventure, greeting you and your compatriots as astronaut recruits and framing his address in explicitly heroic terms. He explains that "You are here to train for the greatest adventure in the history of mankind: the exploration of deep space," and he refers to "...the heroes who went to the moon" in an earlier era of space exploration.[4] By accepting Capcom's Call to Adventure, you are, in effect, agreeing to perpetuate the legacy of the astronauts who preceded you while advancing their ideals and bestowing the rewards of your Journey on all humanity. In this way, you will be serving a greater good — the true mark of a mythic hero.

Following a quick overview of the X-2 Deep Space Shuttle, Capcom introduces the four flight crew positions — Commander, Pilot, Navigator, and Engineer — and stresses that "...the success of your mission will depend on all of you working together as a team." After yet another opportunity to refuse the Call to Adventure, you proceed to the Inmost Cave.

The threshold to the Inmost Cave here takes the form of the Pre-flight Corridor, which is reminiscent of Kennedy Space Center's "White Room," where NASA's astronauts make their final preparations before entering their spacecraft. Here, you will complete your preparations for the Ordeal beyond...or bail out if you suddenly realize you are not ready to accept the Call to Adventure after all.

Capcom appears once again via video to offer final instructions and assign specific tasks to each member of your team. But he is no longer referring to your adventure as a "training" experience. Instead, since the training

---

[4] In 1969, when Apollo 11 astronauts Neil Armstrong and Edwin "Buzz" Aldrin became the first humans to walk on the moon, they left behind a plaque proclaiming, "We came in peace for all mankind." This plaque is the quintessential expression of the idea of the hero acting for the benefit of the greater community — in this case, the entire human race — despite the tremendous personal risk involved.

exercise has now officially begun, everything about your mission from this point forward will be presented as authentic. As the stirring background music reaches its climax, Capcom wishes you "good luck" and the Pre-flight Corridor doors swing open. Beyond, the Inmost Cave beckons.

Once you are secured in your seat aboard the X-2 Flight Trainer and the hatch has been sealed, the voice of Launch Control is heard over the flight deck radio, announcing the final seconds of the countdown. At the same time, you feel your ride vehicle tilt backwards until you are on your back, facing upward while the top of the gantry tower pivots into view on the cockpit screen. Then Launch Control confirms "Lift off!" and you feel the g-forces on your face and chest as your vehicle appears to rise skyward. Your Supreme Ordeal, it turns out, contains its own threshold crossings…and this is the first one.

Pivotal events in your adventure now occur in quick succession as Launch Control hands off responsibility for your flight to Capcom in Mission Control and you rocket past the International Space Station (still looking good after all these years) and out of Earth's gravity well for a "slingshot" maneuver around the moon. Soon the moon's ancient cratered surface is rolling by at phenomenal speed and the fragile blue orb of the now-distant Earth suddenly swings into view. It is a startling reminder of how far your Journey has already taken you from your Ordinary World.

But there's no time for Earth-gazing as Capcom tells the Engineer to "…activate hypersleep" and your metabolism is lowered to a deathlike level for the long journey to Mars. This, however, will not be your only brush with death—nor your only resurrection. You "awaken" in Mars space three months later (though it feels like only two seconds have elapsed) to find yourself in the midst of a massive meteor storm. Quick evasive maneuvers prevent your spacecraft from becoming a mass of mangled space debris, but more near-death experiences await you. They include the failure of your ship's landing autopilot and the overshooting of the landing strip, which almost sends you crashing over the edge of a vast Martian canyon. In each case, cool-headed teamwork by you and your fellow astronaut trainees saves not only the spacecraft and the crew, but the mission itself.

At last, Capcom and the entire Mission Control crew appear on the viewport screen to congratulate you as the words "Mission Accomplished" flash over their image. You have survived your Supreme Ordeal, repeatedly overcome death, and seized your rightful reward (the recognition that you have what author Tom Wolfe famously called *"the right stuff."*)

But as you exit your X-2 Trainer and triumphantly make your way down the long Post-flight Corridor, new challenges await you in the Advanced Training Lab— challenges that will test whether you have absorbed the lessons of your Hero's Journey. They include Mission: SPACE Race, a Mission Control training exercise in which two teams must race against each other to be the first to successfully guide its X-2 Deep Space Shuttle home from Mars. As in your training flight, teamwork and cooperation will be the keys to success. Another Mission Control training experience, Expedition Mars, challenges you to direct a virtual astronaut to safety through Martian dust storms and other hazards.

With your Hero's Journey finally drawing to a close, it is time to return to the "Ordinary World" of Epcot's Future World East. But your initiatory adventure has transformed you, revealing heroic qualities you may only have suspected were present. As a newly minted member of ISTC elite astronaut corps, your taste in clothes, accessories, and even food may have also evolved to match your new status. Happily, the Mission: SPACE Cargo Bay retail venue is well-stocked with an assortment of ISTC and Mission: SPACE logo gear, clothing, and merchandise...and even such "space food" items as freeze-dried ice cream.

A Hero's Journey can contain several smaller Hero's Journeys. In this case, there is a nearly complete Hero's Journey embedded in the Supreme Ordeal stage (the ride experience) of Mission: SPACE. At the same time, the entire Mission: SPACE adventure functions as one part of a larger Hero's Journey outside the scope of the attraction. If the story were to continue beyond your simulator-based "training flight," you would next find yourself crossing the threshold into the Special World of the ISTC astronaut training program to begin your first year as a "rookie astronaut" preparing for your actual mission to Mars.

What of the shadow figure in Mission: SPACE? At first glance, it would seem there is none; everyone at the ISTC appears to be pulling for you to succeed. But on closer analysis, we find there are actually *several* shadows: the X-2 Flight Trainer (the ride vehicle) is composed of some common fears: fear of dark, enclosed spaces...fear of spinning, amplified g-forces, and other unaccustomed sensations...fear of loud noises. The second shadow, within the context of the training simulation, is nature itself— chiefly, the unforgiving environment of outer space and the mysterious, menacingly alien nature of the Red Planet. Although it isn't addressed in the attraction, the history of Mars exploration is littered with a disproportionate number of failed missions, leading some space scientists to jokingly refer to a "Mars Curse" and the existence of a "Great Galactic Ghoul." At three different points during your own voyage to Mars, it seems that the notorious "curse" is about to claim another mission: first, when the X-2 encounters the meteor storm; then, moments later, when the landing autopilot cuts out; and finally, when your spacecraft overshoots the landing strip and is almost sent plummeting to the bottom of the Martian canyon.

Of course, none of these near-disasters is "genuine." In the context of the attraction storyline, they are all merely tests (albeit highly stimulating ones) designed by the ISTC training staff to gauge your team's suitability to join the organization's elite astronaut corps. Therefore, the main shadow figures turn out to be Capcom and his associates, who double as threshold guardians as they contrive a Supreme Ordeal that will once and for all separate the true heroes from the pretenders. In the same way, Capcom also wears the mask of the trickster, tossing one pulse-quickening obstacle in your path after another to see how you'll react.

Altogether, Mission: SPACE doesn't just fulfill its promise to give you an exceptionally realistic taste of space travel; it also launches you into one of the most compelling and immersive expressions of the Hero's Journey ever Imagineered.

Leaving No Swash Unbuckled
Pirates of the Caribbean

THE DISNEY THEMESCAPES ARE LOADED WITH ATTRACTIONS that have rightfully earned the status of "classic." But few are as iconic and beloved as Pirates of the Caribbean. Since its debut at Disneyland in 1967, the ride's resident scalawags have spread out across land and sea to invade the Magic Kingdom-class parks in Orlando, Tokyo, and Paris.[5] All four versions are different from one another in ways both minor and significant. For the purposes of this mythic case study, however, we will focus on the Walt Disney World incarnation. Though it is markedly abbreviated compared to the original Disneyland edition, the Florida version of Pirates nevertheless contains many, if not all, of the most important story beats of its Anaheim predecessor.

The idea that Pirates of the Caribbean tells a story contrasts with the popular notion that there is no real narrative thread running through the experience. Indeed, it is often claimed that the attraction is merely a loose collection of entertaining vignettes tossed together without the benefit of a recognizable story structure. After all, as the ghostly voice that echoes through the grotto asserts, "Dead men tell no tales." But then the infamous pirate Blackbeard, appearing as a waterfall projection, insists that dead men *do* tell tales, adding, "Aye, and tales there be a-plenty in this cursed place..." The overall story becomes especially clear when you view the attraction through the lens of the Campbellian Hero's Journey.

---

[5] And they may eventually arrive in Disney's Hong Kong and Shanghai parks, if some of the more persistent Internet rumors have any truth to them.

As is the case with many other Disney adventures, you begin your Journey through the mythic domain of Pirates of the Caribbean before you have even set foot inside the attraction building. In entering Adventureland from the castle hub, you leave the Ordinary World of Main Street, U.S.A. behind to find yourself in a Special World of unexplored jungles and tropical ports-o-call. Venture deeper into this exotic realm and you'll soon arrive in Caribbean Plaza, with its colorful, tile-roofed buildings evoking the colonial seaports that dotted the islands of the West Indies during the 17th and 18th centuries.

The distinctly Caribbean architecture, color scheme, landscaping, signage and graphics, accompanied by a swashbuckling background music score, serve to smoothly transition you from the South Seas-themed setting of the neighboring attraction, Walt Disney's Enchanted Tiki Room. In this way, Caribbean Plaza is a Special World within the Special World of Adventureland, complete with an "import shop" filled with precious booty and a dining spot where you and your fellow buccaneers can feast on hearty "pirate grub." Though you may come upon the occasional buccaneer elsewhere around Adventureland and the Magic Kingdom (many of them "new recruits" sporting pirate makeovers from The Pirates League salon), you'll find that Caribbean Plaza is their prime stomping ground. By crossing the threshold into this haven of villainy, treachery, and ne'er-do-well cads, you have accepted your first Call to Adventure before it was even issued. And the fact that you feel at home in this nefarious setting speaks volumes. Aye, perhaps ye have a bit o' pirate blood runnin' through yer veins?

The most prominent building in Caribbean Plaza is El Castillo ("The Castle")—a sturdy-looking Spanish citadel that serves as the attraction façade. Attached to the citadel and overlooking the Plaza is the Torre del Sol ("Tower of the Sun")—a sun-bleached watchtower from which an attentive lookout can alert his brethren inside the citadel should a ship flying the Jolly Roger appear on the horizon. But the early warning system has apparently proven insufficient, as the place has clearly been overrun with pirates and the watchtower now stands deserted.

The attraction marquee, emblazoned across a black sail strung from a ship's mast, stands alongside the citadel entrance. It's the closest thing you will get to an official Call to Adventure outside the attraction. But this Call comes with an ominous warning: atop the mast is a weathered crow's nest crewed by a spyglass-wielding skeleton. It's not just a preview of the experience awaiting you beyond the next threshold; it's also a hint of the grim fate that may befall those who succumb to the temptations of a pirate's life.

Cross the threshold of the citadel and you are soon navigating the labyrinthine network of dungeons and arsenals that comprise the interior queue. The dimly lit stone corridors are lined with weapons including muskets, flintlock pistols, and cannons, along with powder barrels, supply crates, ship parts, and jugs of rum—in short, exactly the sorts of items you'd expect to find in a well-stocked fortress of the period.[6] The detailed and slightly spooky environment represents yet another Special World within a Special World, a brain scripted space that smoothly shifts you into a darker mood as it begins to establish the tone of the adventure awaiting you. But even though this is a

---

[6] One dungeon cell contains a pair of pirate skeletons frozen in the midst of an endless chess match. But they are only visible to guests in the separate FASTPASS+ queue and not to Standby guests.

shadowy, cave-like environment, you have not yet entered the Inmost Cave. That part of your Journey still lies ahead.

The murky citadel corridors eventually lead you to a dock situated on a rocky beachfront. Though you are once again "outdoors," you are no longer in Caribbean Plaza. And regardless of the time of day when you entered El Castillo, it is now nighttime here in the place known as Pirate's Bay, at the entrance to a craggy grotto—yet another threshold crossing. Moments later, a flat-bottomed bateau glides to a stop alongside the dock, and a host garbed as a pirate deckhand beckons you and your fellow swabbies aboard.

As quickly as you and your crewmates can settle into your berths and without so much as an "anchors aweigh," your bateau leaves the dock and the current silently carries you through the mouth of the grotto and into the Inmost Cave of your Journey. To your right, through an opening in the grotto wall, you can see a pirate ship anchored further out in the bay, silhouetted against the moonlit sea. Drifting deeper into the cavernous space, you come upon waterfalls spilling into the surrounding pools amidst the menacing stalactites and stalagmites.

The cascading sound mingles with a ghostly voice that echoes the immortal words, "Dead men tell no tales...." And then, on one misty waterfall directly ahead of you, the fierce visage of Blackbeard materializes to contradict the echo, adding, "If ye be brave or fool enough to face a pirate's curse, proceed." With these words, Blackbeard fulfills the mythic roles of both the herald archetype and the threshold guardian. His warning of "a pirate's curse" is especially worth noting, as it will prove to be a key element in your Journey. Indeed, the admonition serves to establish the challenge at the heart of your Supreme Ordeal: you will enter the Special World of the pirates; you will become immersed in their debauchery as they pillage, plunder, rifle and loot; and yet you must ultimately escape the dreaded pirate's curse to return safely to your Ordinary World.

The beach of Dead Man's Cove awaits you as your bateau continues its voyage through the grotto, with the brief stretch of sand illuminated by moonbeams spilling through openings in the catacomb ceiling. You suddenly notice a slight disturbance in the water around you, and if you look over your vessel's gunwales you'll see the shimmering tails of a pair of mermaids swimming alongside the bateau while an alluring siren song wafts through the air. Seconds later, the shapes vanish into the inky depths. But beguiling as they may be to look upon, mermaids are rarely a good omen (notwithstanding the well-known charms of a certain little mermaid who inhabits an attraction elsewhere in the Magic Kingdom). In many myths, sirens not only portend doom for unlucky seafarers, but they are happy to also serve as the instruments of that doom, as the ancient Greek heroes Jason and Odysseus each discovered. In this respect, the mermaids that dwell in the waters of Dead Man's Cove serve as both mythic heralds and as tricksters (just as they did onscreen in *Pirates of the Caribbean: On Stranger Tides*, the movie that inspired this scene). Are they also part of the curse of which Blackbeard spoke moments ago?

As you pass Dead Man's Cove, you come upon a beach littered with the skeletons of pirates who have previously fallen prey to the pirate's curse—all skewered through their ribcages with cutlasses. Another set of skeletal remains unmistakably belong to a mermaid, still bound to the decaying rowboat in which she perished. Is she another victim of the infamous pirate's curse? It's anyone's guess. (Evidently, dead mermaids also tell no tales.)

Before you have time to further ponder the unfortunate mermaid's fate, your bateau carries you into the storm-swept waters of Hurricane Lagoon, where a skeleton skipper clutches the wheel of his crumbling ghost ship as he pilots it through torrential rain, howling winds, and blinding flashes of lightning. The pirate's curse has apparently condemned this fellow to ply the storm-tossed seas for eternity—always within sight of safe harbor but never able to reach it.

If, as the saying goes, "the past is prologue," then perhaps the converse is likewise true and these skeleton scenes offer a glimpse of the fate that will befall the scallywags you'll be meeting in the vignettes still ahead. All that pillaging and plundering, which you will soon witness for yourself, carries a heavy cost, and the attraction's "effect-and-cause" narrative structure allows you to preview the macabre outcome before it happens.[7]

But now another threshold crossing awaits you just ahead. Though the term "threshold plunge" may be a better description, as the transition involves a sudden drop over a short waterfall in total darkness. Feel free to scream along with your crewmates.

Your drop over the waterfall has not only transported you to a new setting, but back in time as well, where you will now witness some of the events leading up to the earlier grotto scenes. And so, leaving the catacombs behind, you arrive in a tropical harbor in the midst of a pitched nighttime battle as a pirate ship anchored just offshore exchanges canon-fire with the defenders inside a besieged Spanish fort (possibly the same citadel where your Journey began minutes earlier). The unseen defenders are the first of

---

[7] In the Disneyland Paris installation, the sequences are arranged in a more chronological fashion, with the grotto and skeleton scenes presented near the end of the ride.

several heroes you will encounter during your voyage. Unfortunately, at this moment you happen to be drifting directly between the opposing combatants. Worse yet, every cannonball that falls short of its target lands perilously close to your bateau, signaling that your Supreme Ordeal is now underway. And even though you are no longer in the grotto, within the structure of your Hero's Journey you are still very much inside the Inmost Cave.

To your relief, the harbor current carries you out of the danger zone before you and your compatriots can become collateral damage. In the course of your Ordeal so far, you have gleaned an important piece of the overall narrative, shouted by the pirate ship's captain, whom you may recognize from the *Pirates of the Caribbean* movies as Hector Barbossa. "It's Captain Jack Sparrow we're after, and a fortune in gold," Barbossa yells, furiously waving his cutlass. "Surrender Captain Jack Sparrow or by thunder we'll burn this city to the ground!"

Now you come upon a new scene as you enter the seaport town of Puerto Dorado[8], where a second pirate captain is taking entirely too much pleasure in his interrogation of "Carlos," one of several local officials lined up for questioning. For poor Carlos—identified by the Imagineers as the local magistrate—it turns out to be a fully immersive experience in the worst possible sense, as the surly pirate captain has him repeatedly lowered into the town's well. "Where be Captain Jack Sparrow?" snarls the interrogator between dunkings. "Speak up—or do ya' fancy a swim with Davy Jones?" But Carlos is resolute, declaring, "I am not chicken. I will not talk—I will not talk!"

---

[8] The town's name is never mentioned during the ride experience—at least not in the Magic Kingdom version—but is reportedly indicated in some of Walt Disney Imagineering's project documents.

Carlos turns out to be another one of the several heroes to be found in the attraction. As we learned earlier, the definition of a true mythic hero begins with the twin ideals of service and sacrifice. Carlos is distinguished by his willingness to forfeit his own well being to protect someone else's. In this case, that someone else is Captain Jack Sparrow, whose location Carlos defiantly refuses to give up to the invaders. He is, after all, the town magistrate—an official who has taken a solemn oath to uphold the laws of his community.

Jack watches all this impassively from a nearby hiding place—visible from your bateau, but unnoticed by the cruel interrogator and his dastardly crew. However, he does absolutely nothing to intervene and seems perfectly content to allow a noncombatant to suffer for his sake. (Jack may later come to the magistrate's rescue, but if he if does so, it's an action that takes place "offstage," entirely outside the existing attraction narrative, and is never indicated at any point during the remainder of the ride.) Then again, the Hero's Journey is a transformational journey. So perhaps you are meant to see Jack at this point in the story as a self-serving cad, only to later witness his emergence as a noble, selfless, and heroic figure? (Hint: Don't hold your breath.)

Leaving the well scene behind, you glide into the town's waterfront Mercado, arriving in the midst of a curious event. The handwritten banner says it all: "AUCTION – Take a Wench for a Bride." A smooth-talking pirate auctioneer presides, gamely parrying the drunken jeers from the audience of heckling brigands. As for the half-dozen "wenches" on the block, a few seem surprisingly unperturbed about their fate. One—"the red-'ed"—is clearly reveling in all the attention, prompting the auctioneer to admonish her to "Strike yer colors ya' brazen wench," and adding, "No need to expose yer superstructure."

The scene is played for laughs, but it presents an intriguing dichotomy that speaks to the odd allure of the pirate's life. In a single moment, you are witness to an event that is both depraved and civilized. By any definition, the auction amounts to human trafficking—a vile and criminal act. Yet it *is* an auction, with the pirate auctioneer steadfastly adhering to a strict set of principles and standards—the bulwark of any civilized society.

The same paradox applies to the piracy business overall. While the pirates of yore were renowned for their lawlessness, they were simultaneously bound by the "articles" of their profession—a collection of rules, regulations, and codes of conduct dictated by their felonious community. Any pirate worth his doubloons would be expected to look after the safety and welfare of his shipmates—a commitment to service very much in keeping with the mythic hero archetype, even when applied to a band of bloodthirsty villains.

Pulled by the inexorable current, your bateau soon arrives in Puerto Dorado's town center, where several of the invading pirates are seen attempting to make off with assorted personal valuables belonging to the local townsfolk—only to be pursued by angry *señoras* and *señoritas* armed with brooms, kitchen implements, and garden tools. But there is no sign of the town's men. Where are they and why have they left the women to defend against the looters? Perhaps they are back in the fort, still exchanging canon fire with the offshore pirate ship? Or maybe they have been rounded up for interrogation like poor Carlos, the now very soggy town magistrate, and his colleagues? Or perhaps they are currently regrouping somewhere outside of town and are now awaiting the opportunity to retake the seaport?

There's plenty of fodder here to feed your speculative impulses, but no actual answers. Instead, you are treated to another glimpse of Captain Jack Sparrow as he stealthily peers out of a barrel, conveniently positioned behind a portly pirate brandishing the key to the town's secret treasure vault along with the treasure map. How do you know what these items are for? Because the tipsy fellow happily declares, "Here I be, holdin' the treasure map and the key as well." Then, with a drunken slur, he adds, "What I wouldn't give to see the look on Captain Jack Sparrow's face!" (The look on Jack's face, which you can easily see from your bateau, is one of surprised pleasure at this unlikely stroke of good luck.)

Once again, Jack receives the heroic Call—the opportunity to leap into action and help the citizens of Puerto Dorado defend their seaport town from this ruthless band of marauders. But once again he refuses the Call, opting instead to pursue his own selfish interests and leaving the task up to the local ladies, who seem far more willing to don the mantle of the hero and assume all the personal risks that come with that role.

As you round the bend leading into the next scene, you are greeted by the strains of a very famous song as a trio of singing pirates belts out a rum-soaked rendition of "Yo Ho (A Pirate's Life for Me)," accompanied by a braying donkey and a barking pooch. Other pirates drunkenly sing along while reveling in their destructive handiwork as the town goes up in flames all around them. For the clueless pirate crew, the growing inferno may be a preview of the fate awaiting them (history has shown that pirates of that era seldom expired from old age). For you and your fellow adventurers, the conflagration brings you to the apex of your Supreme Ordeal, as it seems that pesky pirate's curse may have finally caught up with you.

The drunken carousing fades into the background as your bateau carries you into a waterlogged dungeon, where the cells are occupied by incarcerated pirates eager to escape the encroaching flames. The jailers, like the other men of this town, are nowhere to be seen. Instead, the hoosegow's hound has been left in charge of the prisoners and keeps the jail's single key clamped securely in its jaws. A few of the inmates are attempting to bribe the pooch. But the pup is clearly taking its duties as the jail's unofficial threshold guardian quite seriously, and the large bone offered by the hopeful captives, tempting though it may be, is hardly sufficient to shake the mongrel's resolve. Though it is starting to look like you may escape the pirate's curse after all, it seems these particular rapscallions won't be so lucky.

Moments later, you enter the final scene in your voyage through the Inmost Cave of the Special World of Pirates of the Caribbean: the town's Treasure Room—a chamber packed with a fortune in gold, jewels, and chests heaped with valuables. In the center of the room, Captain Jack Sparrow lounges in a chair fit for a king. Drunk on success and rum, he waves a golden goblet in one hand and studies a priceless bauble in the other. "A toast to piracy and its many shiny rewards," he says, obviously sloshed to the gills. "As a career, what could be more rewarding? Drink up me hearties, yo ho!"

Connecting the dots, you can safely assume that Jack has somehow managed to get his hands on the key and map that had been so avidly sought in the earlier scenes. The apparent message seems to be that crime ultimately *does* pay. Jack even confirms this perception, announcing, "I humbly accept this magnificent treasure as my reward for a life of villainy, larceny, skullduggery and persnickety-nee." Yet how far will that "reward" finally take him? Will he also be claimed by the pirate's curse and ultimately end up as a skeleton on the beach of Dead Man's Cove? It's anyone's guess. But at least you and your bateau-mates are departing the Inmost Cave with your honor and integrity (not to mention your lives) still intact.

Finally, after stepping ashore at the unload dock, you are once again addressed by the disembodied voice of Blackbeard "The fates have spoken, and guided you well," says the voice as you ascend the upramp. "Till we meet again!" Thus begins the Return movement of your Journey, as your adventures in the Special World of the Pirates of the Caribbean continue.

The first station of your Return, in familiar Disney form, is a retail shop—Plaza del Sol Caribe—which is stocked to the rafters with all things piratical. Many of the items are inspired by the ride, and others are inspired by the movies inspired by the ride. The shopping opportunity gives you a moment to pause, catch your breath, and regain your bearings, as is typical at this point in many renditions of the Mythic Round. It also provides you with a chance to take home a souvenir of your adventure—a reminder of the experiences you encountered moments ago and, again, a very familiar element in the Hero's Journey paradigm. You can even "seize the sword" (a chrome-coated polystyrene cutlass, in this case) to bring back with you to the Ordinary World.

Even after you exit the gift shop, you are still in the Special World of Caribbean Plaza as the Return movement of your Journey continues. And, in keeping with the transformational nature of the monomyth, you are no longer quite the same person you were when you embarked on your Journey a short while ago. Though you have (probably) not become a rascal or scoundrel or villain or knave, you may find that your tastes have changed. Perhaps you have the urge to sup like a pirate. If so, follow your nose across the plaza to Tortuga Tavern, where the "Code of Conduct" posted at the entrance warns, among other things, "Damages unto an establishment shall be paid in gold, doubloons, or pieces of eight." (Graffiti scrawled beneath the warning adds, "Parrots be not legal tender." Below that, "Ye be warned." And below that, "No monkeys." You get the idea.)

If you desire to change your appearance to better match your new piratical outlook, you can check into The Pirates League for a head-to-toe pirate makeover, complete with eye patch, fake battle scars, and temporary tattoos. You'll even be given an "official" pirate name. And on a nearby open-air stage, young swashbucklers are invited to hone their sword fighting skills at Captain Jack Sparrow's Pirate Tutorial, where they will be mentored by Captain Jack himself.

The versions of Pirates of the Caribbean currently running in the California and Florida parks are not the same as those that opened in 1967 and 1973 respectively. The current incarnations reflect changes that were introduced into the attractions in the wake of the overwhelming box office success of *Pirates of the Caribbean: The Curse of the Black Pearl* (2003) and its sequels. The updates not only serve to more closely connect the ride to the movies, but also help improve the attraction's narrative cohesion, in turn strengthening its mythic resonance.

Among the most important of these changes, from the standpoint of the Hero's Journey, is the addition of the waterfall mist screen effect early in the grotto sequence, during which Blackbeard invokes the "pirate's curse." This is a story element that may have been subtly implied in the ride's earlier incarnation, but its specific articulation in the current version lends the experience much of its mythic thrust. In essence, Blackbeard is laying down a challenge:

Can you immerse yourself in the Special World of the pirates without bringing the curse down on your head?

Much of the action in this version is motivated by the ruthless pursuit of gold, and that precious metal proves to be a major theme in the attraction. It is certainly a key to the ride's "curse." Captain Barbossa and his pirate crew are keen to plunder Puerto Dorado's hidden treasure cache, and so is Jack Sparrow. Even the name of the pirate-infested town translates to "Golden Harbor" (which, in retrospect, was probably an unwise decision by the town's founders). But in the realm of mythic storytelling, gold inevitably symbolizes far more than material wealth.

Because of its impressive physical properties, gold has always signified perfection and is therefore associated with spiritual purity (a trait which, by definition, a pirate would have in short supply). By the same token, the pinnacle of any civilization is said to be its "golden age." (Coincidentally, perhaps, the attraction's storyline takes place during "the golden age of piracy," which reached its height starting in the 1650s and continued into the 1730s). A person may be said to have "a heart of gold" if his or her flawed external demeanor or behavior belies a hidden heroic nature (which succinctly describes Captain Jack Sparrow's character in the various *Pirates* movies, though this redemptive aspect of his personality is never demonstrated in the ride). This last aspect also speaks to the transformative nature of the Hero's Journey, as your experiences in the Special World bring you more closely in touch with your golden "true self," as distinct from your conscious ego.

Inevitably, your adventures in the pirate domain draw to an end as the siren calls of the other Special Worlds of the Magic Kingdom beckon you to cross new thresholds. And how long will your personal transformation endure following your Journey? That depends on how long your traveling companions can put up with your constant interjections of "Yaaar!" and "Shiver me timbers!" So probably not very long.

.

Yeti or Not, Here We Come!
Expedition Everest

EXPEDITION EVEREST – LEGEND OF THE FORBIDDEN MOUNTAIN
in Disney's Animal Kingdom represents one of the very few
overtly sacred mountains in the Disney themescape (the
others are the various iterations of Big Thunder Mountain in
Orlando, Anaheim, Tokyo, and Paris). It is also one of the
few Disney attractions that explicitly builds a myth into its
storyline and is totally up front about it. Of course, as this
book explains at length, every Disney park, land, and
attraction is filled with mythic content. But only rarely does
an attraction openly identify a myth as the jumping off point
for your adventure. In this case, the myth centers on the
elusive Yeti—the "legend" of the attraction's full title.[9] Of
course, as you'll discover during your Hero's Journey, the
"myth" turns out to be wildly, ferociously true.

The fearsome Yeti, the legendary guardian of the
Himalayas, is believed to inhabit the attraction's eponymous
(and quite fictional) Forbidden Mountain, which you will
travel to, around, over, and sometimes through, on your
way to your final destination—the foothills of nearby Mount
Everest. But be forewarned: the creature is said to have a
nasty temper…and scant patience for intruders.

Your adventure begins in the Kingdom of Anandapur
in the park's Asia section, where the distant Himalayan
mountain range presents a majestic and alluring backdrop.
The range's sacred status is quickly established as you come
upon a *stupa*—a shrine closely replicating the shapes of the
distant mountain peaks. Take a closer look and you'll

---

[9] In the interest of brevity, the attraction will be referred to by its
abbreviated title, "Expedition Everest," through the remainder of
this case study.

discover that the *stupa* encloses a small figure of a ferocious, ape-like creature. This, it turns out, is your first encounter with the Yeti—but it will be very far from your last...assuming you accept your Call to Adventure.

That Call begins to beckon to you as you trek through the Himalayan village of Serka Zong, where the dried-mud roadway is furrowed with tire impressions left by motorbikes and pedicabs. It is issued by the sight of the mountain range in the distance, with its craggy, snow-covered peaks rising above the treetops. Even though you have yet to definitively answer the Call, by now you are already in the Special World of Expedition Everest and have begun to get your bearings in this exotic and exquisitely detailed village with its "third-world" brain script.

The backstory of Serka Zong[10] is that the village was formerly the terminus of a railroad that hauled tea from Anandapur through the Himalayas to markets in other parts of the region. Indeed, you can still make out the rolling hills of green tea plants next to Gupta's Gear, a mountaineering supply shop in the village. For reasons never officially explained, the railroad was abruptly decommissioned. The locals attributed the sudden shutdown to the Yeti fulfilling its role as the guardian of the Forbidden Mountain. The rumors reinforced the long-held beliefs of the area's inhabitants, who have erected various shrines and other expressions of respect for the legendary creature.

In addition to the *stupa*, the most conspicuous gestures of respect in the village are manifested by the strings of *lung ta*—the colorful Tibetan prayer flags that flutter overhead. According to tradition, the flags are intended to carry blessings of peace, compassion, strength, and wisdom to all

---

[10] The name means "Fortress of the Chasm" in the local tongue, according to the Imagineers.

beings everywhere.[11] The *lung ta* are purposefully arranged to frame your view of the Forbidden Mountain as you approach, visually establishing it as a sacred peak.

As your steps bring you closer to the Expedition Everest entrance and the great mass of the mountain range fills the horizon, you are already well into the Separation movement of your Hero's Journey. And now the Call to Adventure becomes audible as the screams of passengers echo through the mountain caverns. The Call is easy enough to accept; all you need to do is step into the offices of Himalayan Escapes, organizers of the popular "Expedition Everest" tour. According to the Imagineering backstory, "Norbu and Bob," the company's proprietors, have "...rebuilt the railroad and repurposed it to transport tourists and adventure seekers to the base of Mount Everest, where they can disembark and climb to the summit." Though Norbu and Bob seem to be selling the tour as a safe and uneventful jaunt through the Himalayas, the name of their business hints at the perilous nature of the excursion, suggesting that somewhere along the way you will have to flee for your life. And you can be sure this won't be the only bit of foreshadowing that you'll encounter as you advance through the queue.[12]

The queue begins in Norbu and Bob's cluttered booking and permit office. A herald in the form of a rusty hand-lettered sign mounted over the office entrance offers an ominous greeting:

> *NAMASTE TASHIDELEK.*
> *Welcome to the Himalayas*
> *Home of the legendary Yeti.*

---

[11] The belief is that, when the *lung ta* are strung at high elevations, the wind blowing through them becomes purified and sanctified by the blessings printed on the individual flags.
[12] For the purposes of this case study, the queue experience will be described from the viewpoint of a standby guest.

Guardian and protector of
the "Realm of the Snows."

The office is in a weathered building that looks as though it may have been standing here for hundreds of years. In a previous life, the building may have even been part of the attached temple complex. Inside, aging office equipment shares space with tourism posters, maps, photos, a few items of expedition gear, and a small shrine. The superimposition of the modern world over a very ancient space is intentionally jarring, and it occurs elsewhere throughout Anandapur and Serka Zong. This uneasy overlap serves an important narrative function, helping to set up the core conflict of the story: What happens when our secular modern world collides with an ancient, spiritual realm? The answer to that question awaits you on the snowy peaks and in the icy caverns of the Forbidden Mountain. But for now, you are still a stranger here as you gradually begin to understand your relationship to this Special World.

The spiritual aspect of that Special World takes center stage as you emerge from the Himalayan Escapes office and immediately find yourself in the "Yeti Mandir," a courtyard-like space occupied by elaborate stone carvings of the Yeti surrounded by recent fruit offerings. A stone shrine features four sculptures of the creature, and there are wall carvings of the Yeti as well. Representations of the creature are even carved into the wooden struts supporting the eaves. Various hand-lettered signs speak to the reverence with which the Yeti is regarded locally. One reads:

Visitors please respect ancient
mandir pagoda which honors Yeti—
protector of the sacred mountain.

From the Yeti Mandir, you next proceed to Tashi's Trek and Tongba Shop where the cheerful-looking sign over the entrance informs you that the establishment provides "...the finest in mountaineer equipments [sic] for all needs new and used." Inside, you again encounter an ancient-looking space cluttered with modern objects—in this case hiking, camping, and mountain climbing gear ranging from boots to pickaxes.

The next doorway leads into the Yeti Museum, where your Meeting with the Mentor takes place. As the sign over the door informs you, the museum is "Dedicated to the serious study of the scientific and cultural aspects of the mysterious creature known and revered throughout the Himalayas as the Yeti." Your mentor is the self-styled Yeti expert, Professor Pema Dorje, Ph.D., who speaks to you not in person but through the museum's exhibit displays, of which he is the curator.

Inside, one wall reveals the museum's previous life as a tea warehouse, with a mural-sized Royal Anandapur Tea Company logo partly obscured by framed photos and captions. There are thousands of display items ranging from newspaper clippings to animal skulls. The exhibits serve to provide you with a deeper understanding of the Special World of the Himalayas. Some focus on the area's geography, geology, flora, fauna, and people, while others examine the widespread belief in the Yeti's existence by "...people of vastly different backgrounds" throughout the region. Indigenous artwork, sculpted idols, and even a ceremonial mask portray the Yeti, often in a spiritual context. One exhibit label reads:

> *This carved wooden statue, recovered from the ruins of the fortress monastery at Serka Zong, represents the Yeti as the "duarapala" or "gateway defender," protecting the mountain from outsiders.*

Of course, having read *Chapter 2: What a Bunch of Characters*, you instantly recognize that this label identifies the Yeti as the threshold guardian archetype of your personal Hero's

Journey. Elsewhere in the museum, you can view a casting of a purported "Yeti footprint" that, according to the exhibit label, has been scientifically evaluated and found to be "anatomically legitimate."

The museum's most alarming exhibit, by far, features a shredded tent and several other items of heavily damaged trekking gear, along with photos and exhibit labels presenting "The Mystery of the Lost Expedition" of 1982. This is an unequivocal warning of the perils that may be awaiting you on your Journey as you penetrate deeper into this Special World. At this moment, your mentor has temporarily donned the mask of the threshold guardian and now seeks to dissuade any wavering would-be heroes from going forward. However, since your heroic impulses are not so easily thwarted, you continue ahead, undaunted.

By the time you reach the museum's exit door, it has become clear that Professor Dorje has taken sides on the question of the Yeti's existence. In a sign posted near the doorway, the curator forthrightly states his convictions and adds a stern note of caution:

RESPECT THE POWER OF THE YETI
THE WEIGHT OF THE EVIDENCE LEADS TO
THE INESCAPABLE CONCLUSION:
THE YETI IS REAL.

You are about to enter the sacred domain of the Yeti, guardian and protector of The Forbidden Mountain. Those who proceed with respect and reverence for the sanctity of the natural environment and its creatures should have no fear. To all others, a warning: you risk the wrath of the Yeti.

Again, the curator has donned the mask of the threshold guardian. However, a second sign posted nearby, handwritten on Himalayan Escapes letterhead, seeks to dispel the dire tone of the professor's message. It reads:

> *The opinions expressed by the curator of the "Yeti Museum" in no way reflect the views of the owners and operators of Himalayan Escapes Tours and Expeditions.*
>
> *- Norbu-Bob, Proprietors*

So who are you to believe? Though the museum contains some highly intriguing "evidence" for the existence of the Yeti, any nagging skepticism you may have would be justified. After all, there is no way to determine how objective the exhibits really are, and the absence of contrary viewpoints only adds to the sense of uncertainty. Ultimately, the curator's parting message removes any lingering doubts about the museum's scientific objectivity...or the lack thereof. As a hero-in-the-making, there's only one thing left to do: climb aboard the tea train and seek out the truth for yourself.

After a brief wait in a corridor lined with posters advertising products such as "Yeti Tea" and "Yeti Brand Muesli," you arrive at the load station, where your refurbished tea plantation train soon arrives. Moments later, with you and your fellow travelers strapped into your seats, your adventure begins.

You quickly leave the village of Serka Zong behind as you cross the threshold into the Himalayan foothills, cruising through bamboo forests as you begin your ascent of the Forbidden Mountain. Even though you are heading uphill, you are actually beginning the Descent movement of your Journey and commencing your Approach to the Inmost Cave. The route includes a steep climb that takes you through the interior of an ancient stone temple— presumably the ruined fortress monastery referred to in one of the Yeti Museum displays. Inside the temple, directly in front of you, a mural depicting the Yeti in his *duarapala* (gateway defender) role warns you, once again, that you are entering a sacred realm.

Of course, at this point the opportunity to turn back has long since passed. And now your train is laboriously chugging up an old iron trestle that precariously straddles the yawning chasm below, while in front of you the mountain's summit grows nearer by the second. At last, cresting the pinnacle, you begin your descent. As gravity takes hold, you are sent swooping through an ice tunnel. You emerge to find that the rails directly ahead have been violently torn out of the rock, their twisted remains silhouetted against the sky. Even the nearby strings of *lung ta* flags are tattered. Your train screeches to a halt just in time to avoid going over the precipice, and as the brakes strain to prevent you from rolling backwards, a bloodcurdling howl echoes off the surrounding crags.

If you take the opportunity to think about it (as you are momentarily left helplessly suspended at the top of the world), this is exactly the sort of fate you had been warned about. No doubt your intentions in making this Journey were pure and your demeanor respectful. Yet the presence of the railway in this sacred place represents a desecration of the mountain, so it should only be expected that the peak's "guardian and protector" would feel provoked to destroy the intrusive structure. And let's be honest: you are hardly an innocent in this whole scenario, as your willing use of the railway, despite numerous admonitions, signifies an implicit endorsement of the sacrilege. Sorry to have to be so blunt about it, but ultimately every hero has to take responsibility for his or her actions, whether or not they are intentional.

Somewhere behind you, a hissing sound mingles with the monstrous howl. Someone—or some*thing*—has just pulled the track switch. Seconds later, the train's overtaxed brakes finally give out and you are sent hurtling in reverse into the inky black network of caverns that honeycomb the upper elevations of the Forbidden Mountain. Collectively, these caverns constitute the Inmost Cave portion of your Journey. As you've no doubt figured out, your Supreme Ordeal is now well underway.

After several tortuous twists and turns, your train screeches to a stop inside the only illuminated section of the cave, where a beam of light casts an alarming shadow on the rocky ceiling. The silhouette of a tremendous, ape-like creature crouches on the silhouette of a length of the track— a literal representation of the mythic shadow archetype. It yanks on the metal rails, easily reducing them to shreds. The creature then appears to notice the intruders (that's you and your fellow passengers, pal) and, with a furious roar, it lunges out of the beam of light and into the darkness.

As if on cue, your train races out of the cavern, speeding forward down the mountain through more ice caverns and dark tunnels with the Yeti's roars following you all the way. Are you hearing the same creature you saw silhouetted a few seconds ago, or are there *several* Yetis lurking along the route, waiting to ambush you? Before you can contemplate either of these equally disturbing scenarios, you plunge into another black tunnel for a final close encounter with the angry creature. In the flickering light of the tunnel, you barely catch a glimpse of the beast—but you can see enough to know that you have evaded his grasp by a mere hair's breadth.

Escaping shaken but unscathed, you laugh in relief as your train exits the tunnel and returns to the safety of the Serka Zong rail depot. And though your expedition to

Mount Everest has been cut short, you begin your Return to the Ordinary World with something far more satisfying: the knowledge that you have come face-to-fang with the legendary Yeti...and lived to tell the tale. More importantly, your harrowing experience may serve to deter others from desecrating the Forbidden Mountain, insuring that this beautiful, rugged realm remains sacrosanct for generations to come. Or at least until the next load of guests climbs aboard your train a few seconds from now. Oh well....

Your final stop as you depart the Special World of Expedition Everest is Serka Zong Bazaar, a rustic souvenir shop decorated with an odd combination of ancient cultural items and contemporary mountaineering gear—a parting reiteration of the "when ancient and modern cultures collide" theme you observed in the queue. Here, and at the in-store PhotoPass counter, you can purchase a souvenir of your adventure—a keepsake to remind you of your Himalayan Hero's Journey.

But who, really, is the hero of Expedition Everest? The answer may seem obvious at first. After all, you've just experienced all four movements of the Campbellian Hero's Journey: Separation, Descent, Ordeal, and Return. Yet the Expedition Everest storyline inverts the relationship between the hero and the shadow archetype—or at least shuffles it up a bit until it is unclear which is which. The Yeti, you are told repeatedly before you board your train, is the "defender" of the Forbidden Mountain. But if you regard a protector figure (one who risks his life to safeguard his community) as a hero, then doesn't this cast you, the intruder, as the source of the story's negative energy, i.e., the shadow archetype?

It is this ambivalence that makes your Journey, based on an ancient myth, into one that is also a modern myth. It's another aspect of the dynamic tension that plays out wherever you find the ancient architecture of Serka Zong overlaid with the trappings of the 21st century...and which makes Expedition Everest ultimately one of Disney's most thought-provoking theme park adventures.

Kiss the Girl
Under the Sea ~ Journey of the Little Mermaid

IN CHAPTER 14: THE BACK SIDE OF WATER, we explored the sacred and primordial energies that mythic heroes encounter when they dive into the seas, lakes, rivers, and lagoons of the Special World to navigate the mysterious depths of their own subconscious. But for Ariel, the title character of Disney's 1989 animated feature *The Little Mermaid*, the ocean deep is also the starting point for a Heroes Journey that has inspired attractions in Disney theme parks in Florida, California, and Japan.[13]

At Disney California Adventure you'll find The Little Mermaid ~ Ariel's Undersea Adventure, which debuted in 2011. The Magic Kingdom version, which opened the following year, is called Under the Sea ~ Journey of the Little Mermaid. Despite their different titles, both feature nearly identical rides. However, the two attractions are set behind very different façades and offer completely different queue experiences. At Disneyland Resort, you approach the load platform through a space that resembles an early 20th century aquarium. In the Walt Disney World version, the exterior façade closely resembles Prince Eric's palace as depicted in the movie, with much of the queue winding through a network of seaside cave tunnels at low tide, which run beneath the castle.

For the purposes of this case study, we will be focusing on the Magic Kingdom version of the attraction. Significantly, the name of this incarnation explicitly

---

[13] Magic Kingdom has two Little Mermaid attractions, Disney's Hollywood Studios and Disney California Adventure each have one, and Tokyo DisneySea has no fewer than six, contained within an entire Little Mermaid-themed land.

identifies the experience as a "Journey." But it's not just Ariel's Journey; thanks to the vicarious nature of the attraction, it's your Journey as well. After all, as the title of this book asserts, "every guest is a hero."

Under the Sea ~ Journey of the Little Mermaid falls into a category the Disney Imagineers refer to (internally, at least) as "book report attractions." Like other "book report" rides, such as Peter Pan's Flight and Pinocchio's Daring Journey, Under the Sea is comprised of key scenes taken directly from the movie.[14] Obviously, the brief running time of the ride required that much of the story be left on the proverbial cutting room floor. As a result, many important scenes from the movie are missing from the attraction, leaving it up to you, the guest, to fill in the gaps between the highlights, using your memories of the animated feature. Nevertheless, the attraction contains enough mythic content and other brain scripted elements to make an analysis worthwhile.

Your Hero's Journey begins on terra firma, as your exploration of Fantasyland brings Prince Eric's tile-roofed castle into view—the most prominent feature of his idyllic seaside kingdom. Situated at the edge of a sparkling lagoon where several picturesque waterfalls cascade over limestone grottos, the Mediterranean-style palace offers an inviting Call to Adventure.

Drawing nearer, you soon come to the bow of a beached sailing ship, which is decorated with a familiar-looking figurehead: a perfect wooden replica of Ariel. Even

---

[14] This is in contrast to attractions such as Toy Story Midway Mania, Indiana Jones Adventure: Temple of the Forbidden Eye, and Roger Rabbit's Car Toon Spin, which send the familiar characters from the movies on all-new adventures. Other Disney attractions, such as Haunted Mansion and Jungle Cruise, are original to the parks.

though you have yet to set foot inside the queue, the show's storyline is already starting to unfold. Here, the implication is that Prince Eric (or perhaps some unnamed mariner from his kingdom) had spotted Ariel at some earlier, but relatively recent, point in her life and was inspired to carve this figurehead. Assuming the figurehead predates Ariel's relationship with Prince Eric, the set piece conveys a sense of pre-destiny for both Ariel and her prince. As mythologist Joseph Campbell occasionally noted, the Fates tend to endow heroes with the adventures they require at a given point in their lives. On another level, the broken vessel and its comely figurehead serve a narrative function, clueing you in to the nautical nature of your forthcoming Journey while also introducing you to the attraction's hero and title character. (And if you really want to take your imagination out for a swim, you may be tempted to speculate as to whether this set piece symbolically presages Ariel's future status as nothing more than a royal "figurehead" in Prince Eric's kingdom. But we digress....)[15]

The Separation movement of your Journey begins as you enter the standby queue, leaving the Ordinary World of the surrounding Enchanted Forest district of Fantasyland behind. Moments later, you are winding your way through a network of seaside caverns at low tide, with seashells and even starfish visible on the tunnel walls and walkways amid the debris of one or more shipwrecks, while waterfalls playfully splash into nearby catch pools. But even though you are in a cave environment, this is not the Inmost Cave. That part of your Journey is still ahead of you. However, it *is* arguably your Approach to that Inmost Cave, complete with

---

[15] It's also possible to read this set piece as post-dating the events in the attraction, with the figurehead carved sometime after Ariel's heroic Journey in tribute to her inspiring story.

a series of tests intended to gauge your suitability for the Ordeal ahead.

Those "tests" are comprised of an amusing little game in which you use a simple gestural interface to direct several busy animated crabs to keep or discard various items that have washed ashore following a recent storm. The crabs appear in the nooks and crannies of the cave at several points along the queue. At first glance, the game appears to be nothing more than mere entertainment—a simple diversion intended to keep you and your fellow adventurers amused as you progress through the standby queue. But if you look at it through the lens of the Hero's Journey, you'll recognize that the crab game's underlying purpose is to establish your ability to communicate and interact with the local marine fauna—a relationship that will prove to be central to Ariel's Journey…and, by association, your own.

Moving deeper into the cavern, you find further proof that your newfound ability to communicate meaningfully with the animal world has taken hold. Now you are actually able to understand a representative of that world—a talkative seagull (who also happens to be a bit of a loon): Ariel's pal Scuttle. Perched on an outcropping inside the cavern, the birdbrain doesn't really have anything of value to share with you; apparently he just likes to hear himself talk. Nonetheless, the fact that he greets you and your fellow adventurers as you pass by is enough to qualify him as a herald archetype. The requirements for being a mythic herald, it appears, are not very strenuous.

Eventually, the tunnel opens up into a spacious stone hall topped with an elaborate vaulted ceiling. Evidently you have arrived in the basement level of Prince Eric's palace, where someone clearly has a bit of an obsession with mermaids. In the dim light of the hanging fixtures, you can barely discern paintings of mermaids covering the ceiling, accompanied by brief rhyming captions. One panel reads:

> *Upon the rocks the sirens call*
> *Has shattered vessels numerous*
> *But bringing sailors to their doom*
> *The sirens find quite humorous*

Obviously, this part of the mermaid legend stands in total contradiction to Ariel's story, as we all know she would never dream of using her vocal talents to lure a boatload of mariners to their doom. On the other hand, the legend itself is very much in keeping with ancient mermaid myths...and with the image of the *siren fatale* presented in Pirates of the Caribbean (both the ride and the fourth movie, *Pirates of the Caribbean: On Stranger Tides*).

Soon the queue leads you to the load area, where a painted backdrop mural depicts Ariel perched on a rock offshore gazing longingly toward Prince Eric's ship at sunset. A steady procession of seashell-shaped ride vehicles glides alongside the load platform, and a friendly attendant directs your party aboard one of them. Seconds later, as the attendant instructs you to "lower your sand bar," your shell carries you through a large opening in the broken stern of Prince Eric's ship, conveying you across yet another threshold into Ariel's Special World.

Moving through the beached vessel, you spot Scuttle again, visible through another breech in the wooden hull and absently playing a concertina (no doubt a piece of washed up cargo he recovered). He greets you as you glide by and then begins to tell you about how "...that evil sea witch almost tricked Ariel's voice away from her." In this capacity, Scuttle again fulfills the role of the herald archetype (this one being of the troubadour variety), welcoming you across the threshold to the undersea realm. At the same time, he frames the rest of your Journey as a flashback as he begins to recount a series of events that have already occurred.

Right on cue, your seashell vehicle rotates until you are moving backward through another large opening in the shipwreck's hull, traveling past a stretch of shoreline littered with washed-up artifacts. Then, with a splash, you feel yourself sinking beneath the waves as the water appears to rise around you. Thus begins the Descent movement of your Journey—both literally and metaphorically.

Soon you are moving through clouds of bubbles, past coral formations and strands of seaweed, as you find the attraction has become "immersive" in more than one sense. The transition, it turns out, is another threshold crossing— this one leading into the submarine world of Ariel and her undersea pals. It's also a trip back in time, to the beginning of Ariel's story.

Finally, you enter an undersea grotto where you catch sight of Ariel and her fine finned friend Flounder, swimming high overhead near the ocean surface beneath an opening in the grotto ceiling. Moments later, you arrive in Ariel's secret undersea hideaway—a chamber of the grotto where she has stashed all the treasures of the surface world that she has collected from various sunken ships. As Flounder hovers nearby, the little mermaid rests on a rock, singing "Part of Your World" as she examines a music box—one of her precious "gadgets and gizmos a-plenty." The items surrounding Ariel—particularly a life-size statue of Prince Eric frozen in a heroic pose—are her Call to Adventure, and the lyrics of her plaintive song express her readiness to accept that Call and act upon it. All of this, of course, is alarming to the little crab Sebastian, who can be seen popping up around the grotto, unnoticed by Ariel.[16]

---

[16] If you have seen the movie, you are already aware that Sebastian is the official court advisor to Ariel's father, King Triton, who has

You see Sebastian again as you leave Ariel's grotto and arrive at a reef, where he conducts a "hot crustacean band" in a high-energy performance of "Under the Sea." Sebastian has now taken on the role of Ariel's mentor, urging her to embrace the status quo as he sings:

> *Darling it's better*
> *Down where it's wetter*
> *Take it from me.*

Though she may not be convinced by Sebastian's song, Ariel is clearly caught up in the music, "dancing" along to the infectious Caribbean rhythms. The rapport she enjoys with her aquatic animal companions isn't surprising. After all, she's half-fish—a state that naturally puts her in close contact with the more primal, instinctual elements of her personality. The sea creatures, meanwhile, provide not just entertainment but also serve as Ariel's allies. During the climax of the movie, they play an important role in helping Ariel overcome the forces of darkness.[17] Speaking of which....

The festive music recedes as your seashell departs the underwater celebration and enters a foreboding submarine canyon, which leads into the spooky lair of the sea witch Ursula. As you approach, the moray eels Flotsam and Jetsam peer out of their shadowy hiding places to whisper enticing words of encouragement calculated to lure Ariel—and you—over the menacing threshold. If the marine animals in the previous scene are Ariel's allies, these two slimy creatures—Ursula's sinister assistants—clearly embody the enemy archetype.

---

dispatched the crustacean to keep an eye on his daughter. If you haven't seen the movie...well, now you know.

[17] Due to the constraints of the attraction storyline, almost the entirety of that climactic sequence is left out of the ride experience.

Having crossed this threshold, you finally arrive in the Inmost Cave, where the tentacled sea witch—embodying the Journey's shadow archetype—happily observes the images that appear within a large crystal globe while she sings a rousing rendition of "Poor, Unfortunate Souls."[18] If you focus on those fleeting images, you'll find they offer glimpses of several key scenes from the movie that are missing from the attraction, including Ariel's post-rescue encounter with Prince Eric on the beach and her more recent signing of Ursula's devious contract in which Ariel unwisely offers her precious voice as collateral in exchange for the opportunity to "be where the people are."

Whether the images in the crystal globe portray events that have already transpired or those still to come, Ariel's interaction with the sea witch in the Inmost Cave signifies her Supreme Ordeal. The fates of Ursula's other clients— reduced to sorrowful, helpless polyps faintly visible in the shadowy crevices of the cavern walls—bring home the gravity of Ariel's ill-considered bargain.

Moments later, you view Ariel's transformation as a bubbling vortex engulfs her while exposing her newly formed legs. Ariel has gotten what she came for, but with some very serious strings attached—and now she and everyone she loves is at risk. The scene demonstrates the transformative nature of the Hero's Journey in a literal way. But the metamorphosis is purely physical—and quite

---

[18] Ursula also fulfills the role of the Shape Shifter, as she is only pretending to help Ariel in her quest to be a part of Prince Eric's world while, in reality, she is actually using Ariel to advance her own wicked agenda. In the movie, her shape shifting proclivities later take on a physical aspect as she transforms herself from a tentacled monster into "Vanessa," a near-doppelganger of Ariel who sings with Ariel's purloined voice.

temporary. Ariel's full and permanent transformation will be signaled by "love's first kiss." But to get to that point, Ariel will first have to prove her readiness to place the welfare of her family and her community ahead of her personal ambitions. In other words, she must become a true mythic hero.

Following a bubbly ascent to the surface world, you arrive at the edge of a romantic lagoon at dusk, where fireflies twinkle and Eric and Ariel prepare to kiss aboard a small boat, encouraged by Sebastian, Flounder, and a chorus of frogs and other aquatic and semi-aquatic creatures singing "Kiss the Girl." All the elements are in place for "love's first kiss." Yet somehow Eric and Ariel's lips never quite connect, signaling that this most important task may be more difficult than Ariel had anticipated.

In the tradition of mythic heroes everywhere, Ariel will ultimately have to put her own future on the line to prevent those she loves from becoming victims of Ursula's diabolical plans. Ariel's heroic deeds, however, will all take place "offstage"—outside the scope of this attraction—leaving you to rely on your memories of the animated feature to fill in the blanks. Indeed, the very next scene skips to the end of the story's climax, with the sea witch visible on the horizon, literally smoldering in fury over her defeat. In the foreground, meanwhile, Ariel and Eric can be seen in silhouette inside a castle doorway. At last the two are kissing—an act that restores Ariel's voice and seals Eric and Ariel's commitment to each other, as signified by a glowing, heart-shaped outline that forms around their heads as they lock lips.

The final scene brings you to the story's finale as the kingdom celebrates the wedding of Prince Eric and Princess Ariel (and presumably the union of two royal families—one terrestrial and the other aquatic). As fireworks explode overhead and King Triton, Sebastian, Flounder, and several other ocean inhabitants look on from the bay, the two newlyweds happily wave from a balcony.

In mythic adventures, weddings are very important events, signifying that the hero has achieved a major milestone in his or her life journey. That's because the act of betrothal involves committing oneself to one's partner. For Ariel, her future is no longer solely about her own ambitions. She is now half of a husband-and-wife team, and a very public one at that. From this point forward, she will be expected to put the interests of her family, the palace staff, and the people of the kingdom ahead of her own, behaving as a true hero must.

As the story's herald, Scuttle gets the last word. Thus, as your seashell ride vehicle returns to the load/unload area, the scatterbrained seagull remarks, "Well they all lived — how does that go? — happily ever after. They also lived in a big castle, which ain't so bad either." But this is not quite the end of the adventure, for you have the option of continuing the story (sort of) just outside the attraction. A few steps from the exit, you'll find the entrance to Ariel's Grotto, a "meet-&-greet" photo opportunity that allows you to spend a few brief moments with Ariel (in her mermaid form) and have your photo taken together. You'll be treated like visiting royalty as you pose for the camera with her, but don't expect Ariel to answer any questions you may have about the mythic aspects of her adventure. After all, at this point in her Journey, she's still trying to figure out the difference between a fork and a comb.

The story of the Little Mermaid, in both the screen and attraction versions, is one of the most literal expressions of the Campbellian Hero's Journey you will likely find within the Disney attractions portfolio. As we learned in Part I of this book, the Hero's Journey resonates with you because it is actually all about *your* life Journey, presented through the metaphor of myth. That Journey, in its most essential form, is the one we all make from a state of childhood dependency to one of adult responsibility—from selfishness to selflessness.

When we first meet Ariel, she is an immature, self-absorbed child. As a mermaid, she has a fish tail instead of legs and she lives her life in a watery realm, breathing liquid. In other words, she is any of us at various points during the first nine months of our existence. She's a fetus in the womb of the ocean—eager to emerge as a fully formed human—to be "part of that world"—but not yet ready to accept the responsibilities that come with that status. As the song says:

> *Flippin' your fins, you don't get too far*
> *Legs are required for jumping, dancing*
> *Strolling along down a—what's that word again?*
> *—Street*

But, as Ariel discovers, it takes more than a pair of legs to become a mature, responsible adult human. Though much of the adventure that gets her to that point is conveyed in your memories of the movie, the attraction version nevertheless touches several of the key events at each end of her Journey and a few in-between. For a Disney dark ride, that's about as much story as you can expect—which, as Scuttle would say, "…ain't so bad either."

Submitted for Your Approval
Twilight Zone Tower of Terror

OF ALL THE DISNEY THEME PARK EXPERIENCES, few can match the iconic presence of Twilight Zone Tower of Terror. The attraction rivals Splash Mountain for the distinction of most compelling Call to Adventure, which here is issued by the screaming passengers briefly visible through the openings high up on the building's ravaged façade.

In fact, Twilight Zone Tower of Terror is all about icons. First, the attraction offers an iconic vision of Tinseltown during the celebrated Golden Age of Hollywood moviemaking. Superimposed over this is the original *Twilight Zone* TV series, a cultural icon in its own right, long hailed for its ingenious and eerily resonant stories. And it's all contained within the foreboding mass of the once-stately Hollywood Tower Hotel, which looms 199 feet over the surrounding themescape.[19]

The first installation of Twilight Zone Tower of Terror opened at Disney-MGM Studios (now known as Disney's Hollywood Studios) in 1994, but the official backstory presents a much earlier origin, with the Hollywood Tower Hotel welcoming its first guests in 1917. According to the backstory (conveyed in the pre-show video), the hotel once stood as "...a beacon for the show business elite"—until the tragic night of October 31, 1939. That's when a freak electrical storm engulfed the glamorous hotel in a

---

[19] Different iterations of Tower of Terror exist at Disney's Hollywood Studios, Disney California Adventure, Walt Disney Studios Park (at Disneyland Paris), and Tokyo DisneySea. But for the purposes of this attraction case study, we will only be analyzing the version at Disney's Hollywood Studios.

mysterious energy pulse, sending an elevator with five unsuspecting passengers plummeting 13 floors toward the hotel basement. Yet the ill-fated elevator cab and its occupants never reached the bottom of the shaft, vanishing mysteriously into the stormy night—along with a sizeable chunk of the hotel building. Sensing something was not quite right, the remaining occupants and staff hurriedly abandoned the hotel, leaving their luggage and other personal belongings behind.

The Hollywood Tower Hotel has remained deserted ever since—a crumbling relic of Hollywood's past. But somewhere within the depths of the decaying edifice, a bank of service elevators is still operational, waiting for anyone bold enough—or foolhardy enough—to embark on a personal Hero's Journey into the furthest reaches of the Twilight Zone.

Rod Serling's famous *Twilight Zone* introductory narration (featured in the attraction's pre-show video) ends with the ominous words: "You've just crossed over into...the Twilight Zone." Not surprisingly, your Twilight Zone Tower of Terror adventure involves a number of threshold crossings, each of which conveys you deeper and deeper into its Special World, until you are finally sent plummeting into a realm "beyond the fifth dimension."

Answering the Call to Adventure extended by the sight of the tower from afar and the screams of those who have embarked on their own Journeys within, you cross the First Threshold, defined by the stone gateway marked "Sunset Hills Estates" at the beginning of the hotel's entry drive. This is the boundary that divides the attraction's Special World from the Ordinary World of Sunset Boulevard just outside the gateway. By crossing this initial threshold, you have commenced the Separation movement of your Hero's Journey. And even though you are barely a stone's-throw from the intersection of Gower Street and Sunset Boulevard, the suddenly lush, overgrown landscaping creates the sensation that you are no longer anywhere near "La-la-land," either in time or space.

A second threshold crossing—this one in the form of an ornate iron gate—separates you from the entry drive and transitions you into the unkempt, neglected, yet still somehow picturesque formal gardens. The gardens are so wildly overgrown in places, they appear to be trying to keep you away from the derelict hotel—a sort of botanical threshold guardian. Out of the tangle of dead and dying vegetation, small age-stained directional signs point to the "Bowling Green," the "Natatorium," and other long-forsaken hotel amenities. In addition to giving you a sense of the geography of this Special World, the signs are a wistful reminder that this was once a place teeming with activity—a lost playground for Hollywood's brightest stars. The feeling of desolation and ruin is reinforced by the cracked and mildewed statues that dot the grounds.

More decrepit conditions greet you as you reach the hotel's Grand Terrace, where the overgrown arbor and the desiccated, cracked reflecting pool deepen the spooky mood. And that's when you catch the haunting strains of a Big Band orchestra, echoing from a distant ballroom in another century—an aural and surprisingly wistful example of the "faded glory" brain script. Now look upward and you'll be treated to a closer view of the screaming guests high up in the tower as they briefly become visible through the scorched wound of the building's devastated façade.

It's all distinctly unsettling, and you may be tempted to refuse your Call to Adventure, turn around, and hurriedly make your way back to the familiar Ordinary World of Sunset Boulevard. Yet your curiosity to discover the mysteries that lie within the Tower of Terror overpowers your natural reticence. Or maybe you're just trying to prove your courage. Either way, you press ahead, determined to confront whatever strange fate may be awaiting you. This, it turns out, was your first test along the Road of Trials. Congratulations—you passed.

A set of impressive bronze doors mark the next threshold crossing—this one leading you into the dusty, long-abandoned hotel lobby. Although the full backstory of the attraction has yet to be communicated (Rod Serling himself will provide that crucial information once you enter the Library), by taking a few moments to observe your surroundings in this part of the Special World, you can begin to gather a few helpful clues on your own. And what you find here is a moment frozen in time—a tableau that includes an unfinished chess match...a pair of champagne glasses (one with visible lipstick stains on its rim)...unclaimed suitcases and steamer trunks slowly rotting at the bellhop station...and other poignant artifacts pointing to a hasty evacuation. Though this hotel may not technically be a "haunted house" (for that, see the Haunted Mansion case study later in this section), there is an aura of death and decay hanging over this place. Again, the surroundings ultimately convey one message: something terrible happened here and you really shouldn't stay if you know what's good for you. On the other hand, you have come too far to turn back.

Presently, you pass the abandoned front desk and approach the lobby's elevator foyer, where the proverbial plot thickens. For one thing, you notice that all the elevator doors are seriously damaged, while the severe cracks in the walls surrounding the doors testify to some sort of horrific "accident." A dusty "Out of Order" sign sums up the elevators' current condition (and, indeed, the status of the entire hotel) with macabre brevity. Glancing up, you can see that the floor indicator arrows over the doors point to a non-existent floor that's inexplicably below basement level. But before you have time to contemplate the forces that could have caused such an event, a cheerfully morose bellhop welcomes you and directs you to the foyer of one of the hotel's two libraries.

When the stately oak library doors swing open, you make yet another threshold crossing to enter the handsome yet gloomily lit room. The walls around you are lined with bookshelves crammed with leather-bound volumes, while fine antiques, curios, and *objets d'art* are scattered among the upper shelves. Look closely and you may recognize a few props from specific *Twilight Zone* episodes.[20] There's also a vintage television set that abruptly flickers to life with a "lost" *Twilight Zone* installment as a flash of lightning extinguishes the room lights.[21]

The episode begins with the familiar *Twilight Zone* title sequence. Then Rod Serling proceeds to narrate the story of that storm-tossed night in 1939 that sent five unlucky passengers plummeting into another dimension. Finally appearing on screen, Mr. Serling directs your attention to a still-functioning maintenance service elevator. "We invite you, if you dare, to step aboard," he says, issuing the attraction's first spoken Call to Adventure. "Because in

---

[20] Those props initially included a pair of broken spectacles from the episode *"Time Enough at Last"* (starring Burgess Meredith), the "Mystic Seer" fortune-telling machine that torments William Shatner in the episode *"Nick of Time,"* and the notorious cookbook from the episode *"To Serve Man."*

[21] The TV appears to be a model from the 1950s. So what's it doing in the library of a hotel that was supposedly abandoned in 1939? Isn't that an anachronism? Then again, you are now in the Special World of the Twilight Zone, so you would be wise to expect the unexpected.

tonight's episode you are the star, and this elevator travels directly to...the Twilight Zone." With another crash of thunder, one of the bookcases slides open, revealing a secret tunnel. But rest assured, you will be hearing from Mr. Serling again. As the mentor of your Hero's Journey, his cool, detached voice will be accompanying you at crucial moments, offering his unique perspective on the strange events that are about to engulf you.

Your excursion through the pipe-lined concrete passage marks the commencement of the Descent movement of your Journey and the Approach to the Inmost Cave: the hotel's dim, steamy Boiler Room, where the muffled sounds of machinery, chains, and heating ducts reverberate amidst the massive furnaces. Although the hotel is supposedly abandoned, a faint orange glow is visible from within the furnaces. Somehow, the hotel's power plant is running unattended — at a minimal level, perhaps, yet to a degree sufficient to power the building's service elevators.

Arriving in front of one of those elevators, you realize that the grimy doors are identical to the ones toward which Rod Serling gestured at the end of the pre-show video a few moments ago. Soon enough, your elevator cab arrives and the doors slide open. A suitably glum elevator attendant then escorts you aboard, accompanied by 21 of your fellow adventurers, and confirms that you are all safely strapped into your seats. The doors slide shut and you are once again joined by Mr. Serling's voice, announcing that you are "...about to ascend into your very own episode of *The Twilight Zone*." The Ordeal movement of your Journey is now underway (with emphasis on the word "movement.")

Your first stop is the fourth floor, where the elevator doors open onto a view of an empty hotel corridor. This is an Inmost Cave within an Inmost Cave. There's a flash of lightning and suddenly the five doomed elevator passengers from the 1939 event materialize before your eyes. The glowing, phantom-like entities gesture to you as another flash of lightning envelopes them in electrical energy and then spreads to the corridor walls. The walls dissolve away, revealing a starry night sky beyond and leaving the window at the far end of the corridor hovering in space. Over the next few seconds, the window warps and transforms into the same window you saw in the *Twilight Zone* title sequence during the Library pre-show video. Replicating the title sequence, the window abruptly shatters just as the elevator doors slide shut.

As your elevator resumes its ascent, you are once again accompanied by the voice of Rod Serling. "One stormy night long ago, five people stepped through the door of an elevator and into a nightmare," the voice informs you. "That door is opening once again, and this time it's opening for you." Right on cue, the elevator doors slide apart to reveal an otherworldly scene: the "Fifth Dimension." Then your elevator cab does what no ordinary elevator can possibly do as it slips quietly out of the shaft and proceeds to move horizontally through a surreal environment where sections of the hotel architecture are interspersed among icons from the *Twilight Zone* title sequence floating against a star-strewn backdrop.

As the show's title music drifts through the air, you pass a door, a window, a clock, and a giant eyeball. You even catch a glimpse of yourself and your fellow passengers reflected in the eye. It is clear that you are no longer a mere observer; from this moment forward, you are very much a part of the story. But before you can contemplate this new reality, the surrounding stars converge to create a thin vertical line. The line splits along its length, forming two vertical edges that pull apart—exactly like an elevator door gliding open. "You are about to discover what lies beyond the Fifth Dimension..." intones the voice of Rod Serling as your elevator cab rolls through the opening, "...beyond the deepest, darkest corner of the imagination—in the Tower of Terror." And then, with no further warning, you are sent plummeting into the darkness below. Thus begins your Supreme Ordeal.

Despite your safety belt, you feel yourself lifted up out of your seat as your elevator cab goes into free-fall, while your screams mingle with those of your fellow passengers.[22] But instead of slamming into the floor of the elevator shaft, your cab abruptly halts and then just as suddenly shoots skyward through the darkness, toward the upper reaches of the tower. There, a set of doors snaps open and you find yourself looking out over the vista of the theme park and the landscape beyond. You pause there just long enough for passersby far below to catch a glimpse of your self-inflicted predicament before you are dropped once again, screaming, into the black abyss. But for that one, brief moment, you are not only immersed in the story—you are a part of the *show*. You and your elevator-mates have become temporary heralds, your screams echoing like a siren's song, luring thrill-seekers within earshot to queue up and seek their own destiny within the Tower of Terror.

After several more harrowing drops and ascents, your elevator at last returns you to the relative safety of the hotel basement. Then, as the cab makes its final deceleration, you are treated to more title imagery from the *Twilight Zone* TV series. At the same time, the disembodied voice of Rod Serling welcomes you back and offers you "...a friendly word of warning—something you won't find in any guidebook: The next time you check into a deserted hotel on

---

[22] Thanks to a set of powerful drive motors, your elevator cab plummets at a top speed of 45 feet per second, which is actually faster than the acceleration from the force of gravity alone.

the dark side of Hollywood, make sure you know just what kind of vacancy you're filling—or you may find yourself a permanent resident of...The Twilight Zone."

As this ominous advice sinks in, the elevator doors open one last time and the Return movement of your Journey begins. You exit from your elevator and head on wobbly legs down another basement maintenance corridor, toward a utility lock-up cage containing several recognizable props from the *Twilight Zone* television series. Above the lock-up cage, two vintage-looking TV sets display photos of you and other passengers surreptitiously snapped during the height (or perhaps the depth?) of your Ordeal. As Rod Serling once commented, "...tangible manifestation is often left as evidence of trespass—even from so intangible a quarter as the Twilight Zone."[23]

Indeed, tokens of one's adventures in the Special World are a familiar element of the monomyth. These mementos of the Journey may take the form of an enchanted sword, a mystical ring, a healing elixir, a holy chalice, a rescued princess, a golden fleece, or any number of other prizes. Following your Tower of Terror adventure, you can commemorate your adventure with a print of your image capture photo ordered from the Picture If You Will... photo counter near the hotel's meeting and banquet rooms. More souvenirs can be found in the adjacent Tower Gifts shop— from monogrammed hotel towels to logo coffee mugs and t-shirts...even front desk bells emblazoned with the Twilight Zone Tower of Terror insignia.

From Tower Gifts, it's only a short stroll to the familiar environs of Sunset Boulevard as you finally arrive back in the Ordinary World. Yet the screams of other elevator

---

[23] From the Season 5 episode "Nightmare at 20,000 Feet."

passengers linger in the air—chilling reminders of your just-completed Hero's Journey to and from the Twilight Zone.

Walt Disney Imagineering's idea of branding Tower of Terror as a *Twilight Zone* experience may have struck some skeptics as puzzling at first. Why theme a thrill ride after a television series that originally aired three decades earlier? Yet the concept proved a winning one. At the time, the series was still entertaining viewers through re-runs (and continues to do so today through streaming online video). More importantly, the show had earned iconic status for its masterful ability to convey its own modern myths. By using the metaphorical language of science fiction and fantasy, Rod Serling and his writers were able to deftly skirt the CBS network censors to address a variety of hot-button topics, including McCarthyism, mass hysteria, and the dangers of nuclear war.[24]

But the attraction also taps into some very ancient myths—especially during the Ordeal movement, when you are sent plummeting into a seemingly bottomless pit by malevolent supernatural forces. The "descent into the underworld" theme occurs so frequently in classical Greek mythology, there's even a name for it: *katabasis*. The convention encompasses familiar Greek myths ranging from the story of Orpheus and Eurydice, to *The Odyssey*. And the first book of the 14th century Italian poet Dante Alighieri's epic poem *The Divine Comedy* (AKA *Dante's Inferno*) follows the author on an allegorical guided tour of the underworld.

Often in myth, the ability of a living hero to descend into and return from the world of the dead—usually in a

---

[24] Those writers included such luminary genre authors as Ray Bradbury, Harlan Ellison, Richard Matheson, George Clayton Johnson, Damon Knight, Lewis Padgett, and Jerome Bixby. Serling, meanwhile, personally wrote 92 of the original 156 episodes.

quest to rescue a loved one or to retrieve an object of special significance—proves that hero's worthiness. Sometimes the prize is the knowledge of what exists beyond the limits of our normal perceptions. But occasionally the reward is simply the wonder and thrill of the Journey itself—from light to darkness and back to light...from life to death and back to life...from hope to despair to hope once again. And it is in this "twilight zone," suspended between extremes, where the greatest adventures occur—as you discover and re-discover every time you drop in on Twilight Zone Tower of Terror.

Get Your Kicks on Route 66
Radiator Springs Racers

IN THE PARALLEL UNIVERSE of Disney-Pixar's 2006 feature *Cars* and its various sequels and spinoffs, the "people" are cars, trucks, forklifts, and the occasional helicopter.[25] What, then, does this make *you* when you visit Cars Land at Disney California Adventure and take a spin on Radiator Springs Racers?

Enter the picturesque town of Radiator Springs and you'll find yourself immersed in a meticulously detailed re-creation of one of the main settings from the first *Cars* movie. At first glance, the place resembles any number of other dusty small towns along a certain stretch of America's iconic Route 66. But upon closer inspection, you realize that all the buildings and accompanying signage are intended for residents and visitors of an automotive persuasion—from Ramone's House of Body Art, to the Cozy Cone Motel, where even the flowers blossoming in the front garden turn out to be vintage auto tail lights. So perhaps it would be best for you to just go with the flow, play along, and pretend that you're a car, too. (Don't worry about feeling silly; trust me — all your fellow visitors are doing the same thing.)

When you entered Cars Land on your way to Radiator Springs Racers, you crossed a major threshold, leaving the Ordinary World of Disney California Adventure behind to enter the Special World of Radiator Springs at the edge of scenic Ornament Valley. You can even see the tailfin-shaped

---

[25] Cows, on the other hand, are tractors, bulls are harvesters (or sometimes bulldozers), and houseflies are (naturally) tiny VW Bugs.

peaks of the Cadillac Mountain Range rising majestically in the distance.

Like many other Disney attractions, your appreciation of Cars Land is enhanced by your familiarity with its cinematic source material. In this case, the fidelity to the onscreen version of Radiator Springs is uncanny, with landmarks such as Flo's V8 Café and Luigi's Casa Della Tires re-created with stunning exactitude. Depending on your timing, you're also likely to encounter Lightning McQueen, Mater, and other life-size automotive characters from the movie rolling along the town's main drag (which looks freshly re-paved, just as it appears onscreen after Lightning completes his community service sentence).

A stone and neon arch topped with the words "GATEWAY TO ORNAMENT VALLEY" (a straightforward reference to its function as a threshold) marks the entrance to the Radiator Springs Racers queue. Traversing this threshold, you enter "Stanley's Oasis" — a ruggedly beautiful Special World within the Special World of Cars Land. As several of the other attraction case studies in this section reveal, it is not uncommon for multiple Special Worlds to be embedded within a larger, overarching Special World.

Stanley's Oasis, you soon learn, is named after the founder of Radiator Springs—the same automobile (a Stanley Steamer, of course) depicted by the statue in front of the Carburetor County Courthouse. The "Original Radiator Spring" splashes from a rock formation that resembles the hood of an antique auto. The spring is surrounded by a fence and supplies an adjacent wooden water tower from which thirsty cars are welcome to replenish their radiators. A rust-streaked metal sign mounted on the water tower frame fills in the backstory:

> *On this site, in the summer of 1909, Stanley,*
> *exploring out west, overheated as his radiator*
> *water boiled away. Coasting into the shade, he*
> *happened upon a life-saving natural spring.*
> *Upon this most fortunate discovery, Stanley*
> *founded the first settlement in Ornament Valley,*
> *and in honor of the oasis, christened it Radiator*
> *Springs.*

Other whimsical signs promote the service station and other facilities Stanley established nearby. One reads, "Stanley Always Has Gas," while another assures visitors that the garage is "Open 8 Days a Week!" However, the largest and most noteworthy sign, at least from a mythic standpoint, is a weathered billboard promoting the curative properties of the water that burbles up from the "...mysterious, world-famous Radiator Spring." This natural spring supposedly "Removes rust," "Stops leaks," "Restores dull paint to [its] original luster," and even "Turns back the odometer."

If the billboard's claims are to be trusted, the Original Radiator Spring is a veritable fountain of youth—a place of sacred healing waters. The legend of the discovery of this remarkable spot presented in the water tower sign, supplemented by the adjacent billboard, is essentially the story of Stanley's own Hero's Journey. The key elements of the classic Heroic Round, though much abbreviated, are right there in the text: Stanley crosses into a Special World (the desert wasteland of Ornament Valley) where he undergoes a Supreme Ordeal, including a near-death experience (he overheats and his radiator water boils away) followed by a resurrection (the natural spring water revives him). The boon he returns with (the spring water, which the billboard refers to as "Nature's Own Fixer Elixer" [sic])—not only delivers benefits to his community (Radiator Springs), but makes that community possible in the first place. Significantly, in many versions of the Hero's Journey, a magical elixir is one of the typical rewards that the hero seizes in the course of, or immediately following, the Ordeal.

Leaving the restorative spring, you come to a collection of covered, open-air buildings that comprise the "Garage in the Mirage" portion of Stanley's Oasis. They include Stanley's Cap-N-Tap radiator cap shop (slogan: "If we don't have your cap—it's free!"), and a service station selling "Butte Gas" brand gasoline out of vintage gas pumps. A third open-air building, identified as "The Amazing Oil Bottle House," features plaster walls embedded with hundreds of empty colored glass oil bottles that filter the sunlight like miniature stained glass windows, adding an unexpected spiritual dimension to the queue. Cactus gardens reinforce the southwestern desert setting while nostalgic auto-themed tunes waft through the air. The numerous details add up to present a brain script that fairly shouts "desert tourist trap."

At last, you enter the mouth of a cavern, which turns out to be the lobby of the Comfy Caverns Motor Court (reminiscent of the Wheel Well Motor Court seen in the first *Cars* movie). The interior signage lists amenities such as "Free Cavern Tours" and "Lincoln Continental Breakfast." But despite its appearance, this is not the Inmost Cave of your Hero's Journey; even in the mythic landscape of the Special World, sometimes a cave is just a cave.

Arriving at the load platform that runs though the middle of the cavern, you await the arrival of your ride vehicle. With its windshield eyes and its smiling front bumper, the sporty six-passenger convertible looks completely at home in the *Cars* universe. But when you climb aboard, you are doing something that has never been seen in any of the *Cars* movies or spinoffs: you are giving the vehicle a passenger. Nevertheless, aside from a brief audio safety spiel from Sheriff, no one acknowledges that you are present—at least not in human form. Instead, from this point onward, you will be addressed as though you are the car in which you are now seated.

Your excursion begins as you pull out of the load cavern and head outdoors for an idyllic drive through Ornament Valley, passing pine trees, driving through a rock tunnel, and catching a glimpse of a lovely waterfall—all accompanied by a relaxing and sometimes inspiring musical score. But even though you are now on the road (Route 66, to be specific) and approaching the Inmost Cave, you are not yet on the mythic Road of Trials. But not to worry; that will change any moment now.

As you round the next curve, the mouth of another cave comes into view. At last, you are entering the Inmost Cave—a literal cave in this case. You plunge into the darkness, barely avoiding a head-on collision with Mack (Lightning McQueen's car carrier). Seconds later, you experience a similar near-collision with tourists Van and Minnie, a pair of wayward minivans. But despite initial appearances, these close calls with disaster are not your Supreme Ordeal. That stage of your Journey is still to come. Instead, these vehicles play the role of the threshold guardians, presenting you with your first tests along the Road of Trials.

But what is the Road of Trials doing inside the Inmost Cave? Isn't that stage of the Hero's Journey supposed to occur during the Descent movement? Usually yes, but not always. As we see in several of the other attraction case studies in this section, the structure of the monomyth is extremely flexible. Stages can be added, dropped, or re-arranged in a nearly endless array of combinations to meet the demands of the story, the whims of the storyteller, and the predilections of the audience. Like a Russian nesting doll, some stories can even feature several subordinate Hero's Journeys within a larger, overarching Hero's Journey.

In the case of Radiator Springs Racers, your entry into the Inmost Cave is where you are tested to determine if you are worthy of continuing onward toward your Supreme Ordeal. By successfully avoiding a collision with the three threshold guardians, you have proven your road-handling skills—an ability that will be essential when your Supreme Ordeal finally begins.

Yet there are still two more threshold guardians you will need to face. First, there's an oncoming train to be outraced (you make it across the tracks in one piece—just barely). And finally, there's Sheriff, who lurches out from behind a billboard with his siren blaring. But instead of writing you a speeding ticket, Sheriff lets you off with a warning and then tells you to follow Mater into town to get ready for the big race.

As in the *Cars* movies and spinoffs, Mater the tow truck serves as the Journey's trickster archetype. And so, as he escorts you into town (driving in reverse, of course), he detours into a nearby pasture to take you tractor tipping. "It's easy!" he assures you. "Just sneak up on 'em and honk. Ready?" Then, as an aside, he adds, "Don't let Frank catch ya'." The sound of your car horn startles a trio of sleeping tractors and sends them falling over backwards. But it also awakens a very angry harvester, which proceeds to charge. "That's Frank! *Ruuun!*" laughs Mater as you flee across the moonlit pasture, toward the safety of downtown Radiator Springs.

Frank, it turns out, is the last of your threshold guardians. Now, as you arrive in town, you are welcomed by Sarge (a military Jeep) and Filmore (a trippy VW microbus) in their roles as heralds. Rolling down the neon-lit main street, you pass other residents of Radiator Springs before coming to Lightning McQueen and Sally, the Porsche. Between them, a sign reads, "Race Today – Check-in Here." Acting as heralds, they welcome you to Race Day before sending you to either Luigi's Casa Della Tires for a tire change or Ramone's House of Body Art for a spiffy new paint job (depending on your timing). In either case, it's all part of the preparations for the big race—your Supreme Ordeal. After all, as Sally and Lightning point out, a true competitor needs to look the part.

But why is that so? Aren't such touches purely superficial? Perhaps not. For the inhabitants of this particular parallel universe, putting on whitewall tires or getting a custom paint scheme may be an effective means for giving one's self a mental edge (i.e., "psyching yourself up") in anticipation of the Supreme Ordeal ahead. You might compare these preparations to the ritual in some cultures of applying war paint before going into battle.

At the same time, these cosmetic changes point to the transformative nature of the initiatory Journey. Indeed, the application of facial and body paint, ceremonial garments, special jewelry, and other decorative features are familiar elements in the rite of passage traditions practiced by cultures around the world. Such external transformations are often used to signify internal ones. And the need for the hero to ultimately undergo an internal transformation is, of course, the point of every Hero's Journey.

Now that you have been spiffed-up, you roll to the starting line for the big race, passing Doc Hudson, who wears a headset and urges you to "pay attention and do us proud." As your crew chief, he will be serving as your mentor during the race, offering sage advice over your radio as you strive to beat the car that waits alongside you. Luigi, the tire shop's namesake owner, provides the countdown and then drops the starting flag.

With engines roaring, you and the competition shoot out onto the twisting mountain racecourse, accelerating around buttes, through stone arches, over camelbacks, past geysers, and down high-speed straightaways. Though you are no longer in the Inmost Cave, this is your Supreme Ordeal. At key moments, your mentor Doc Hudson offers advice and encouragement over the radio, warning you to "Hold tight around the curve!" and later pressing you to "Pour it on!"

After running neck-and-neck with your competitor, you cross the finish line, winning or losing the match by barely a length. (As it happens, the "winner" was randomly pre-determined by the ride control system, though that's really not the point. But we'll deal with that issue shortly.) Whether you win or lose, the voice of Doc Hudson congratulates you as you slowly roll into Tail Light Caverns (a location advertised on the billboard you saw when Sheriff admonished you a few minutes ago). Amid the stalactites and stalagmites shaped like, yes, vintage automobile taillights, you meet Lightning and Mater once again as they offer a few additional comments on your achievement.

So concludes your Supreme Ordeal. Now, as you pull alongside the unload platform, your Journey ends where it began: in the lobby of the Comfy Caverns Motor Court, amidst the ruggedly beautiful landscape and picturesque cacti of Stanley's Oasis. As you follow the walking route back to town, you can enjoy the sight of more racers speeding along the outdoor track while you ponder one lingering question: If everyone comes out of the competition feeling like a winner, what is the point of the race?

Like all Supreme Ordeals, the race portion of your adventure serves to determine whether you have absorbed the lessons you learned during the earlier stages of your Hero's Journey—especially during the "Road of Trials" sequence, when your maneuvering skills and reflexes were honed in a rapid-fire series of near-collisions. Win or lose, your honorable completion of the race signifies that you have accomplished your heroic transformation—that you have passed the rituals of your initiation.

Now, and for the remainder of your time in Cars Land, you can consider yourself a fully vested member of the Radiator Springs community. In doing so, you'll be following in the tire tracks of Lightning McQueen, who underwent a similar—if more prolonged, dramatic, and challenging—transformation in the first *Cars* movie. So congratulations and feel free to toot your own horn. Just don't let Frank catch ya'.

Everybody's Got a Laughing Place
Splash Mountain

WHILE MANY DISNEY ATTRACTIONS can trace their mythic lineage to relatively contemporaneous tales inspired by modern myths, at least one attraction finds its roots in original myths dating back hundreds of years. The key characters and situations you encounter when you ride through Splash Mountain are direct descendants of the anthropomorphized animals and scenarios at the center of native folk tales told long ago by the Yoruba people of Southwestern Nigeria and the bordering sections of Benin and Togo. Those tales were carried to America and passed along to subsequent generations by the plantation slaves of the Old South. Eventually they were retold by journalist and folklorist Joel Chandler Harris in his collection of "Uncle Remus" stories. They later became the basis for Disney's 1946 live-action/animated feature *Song of the South*, which ultimately inspired Splash Mountain.

Though the Uncle Remus character is nowhere to be found in the attraction, you can experience several of the stories attributed to him when you ride Splash Mountain in Disneyland Park, the Magic Kingdom, or Tokyo Disneyland.[26] And while there are subtle but significant differences between the attractions, all three versions send you on a foolhardy adventure with Brer Rabbit—a close relative of the Trickster Hare character and other trickster animal archetypes that are a familiar presence in the mythologies of many cultures.

The fact that the Hero's Journey undertaken by Brer Rabbit is a foolish one is a major aspect of the attraction's

---

[26] For the purposes of this case study, we will be analyzing only the Magic Kingdom version of the attraction.

premise and one that is bluntly singled out several times in the course of the show's narrative. As you'll discover when you join Brer Rabbit on his adventure, the chain of events leading up to your drenching splashdown at the ride's climax amounts to a litany of warnings gone unheeded.

That splashdown—part of the attraction's Supreme Ordeal—doubles as your Call to Adventure as you approach Splash Mountain. Indeed, it may very well be one of the most spectacular Calls of any Disney attraction anywhere. As Walt Disney Imagineering legend John Hench once described it:

> ...guests see riders plummeting down a fifty-two-foot flume chute at a forty-five-degree angle, apparently disappearing into a bank of briars below. Anyone catching sight of this wants to know, How did that happen? Where did they go? What's going on over there? It is very enticing, eye candy.

As for the warnings, those begin within moments of your entering the standby exterior queue, where colorful birdhouses dot the woodsy, shade-dappled path. But these are no garden-variety birdhouses. Rather, they resemble miniature human houses complete with doors, windows, porches, and chimneys. Clearly you have crossed a threshold and are now in a Special World where animals are people. And, if you listen closely, you'll hear tiny, high-pitched voices drifting from the birdhouses. The very public personal life of Brer Rabbit seems to be the topic du jour in this community, and the birds in their tiny houses are chirping up a storm about how that heedless hare is bound for trouble.[27]

---

[27] Biologically, rabbits and hares are different animals belonging to two different families within the order Lagomorpha. But in

The next section of the queue weaves in and out of a barn-like building filled with barrels, supply crates, and farming implements, establishing the rural, agricultural nature of this Special World. The queue then transitions into a network of earthen tunnels. This, it turns out, is the route to Critter Cave, and it's not hard to imagine some of Brer Rabbit's neighbors residing in this subterranean habitat. Sure enough, you soon come upon one of those neighbors as you peer into the cozy underground home of Brer Frog—an apparent stand-in (or sit-in) for Uncle Remus. Though Brer Frog himself is not visible, his presence is made known through his shadow, cast upon a clay wall by hearth-light, and by his voice as he croaks a few words about Brer Rabbit and his misadventures from the comfort of his rocking chair.

Nearby, a pair of framed needlepoints mounted on the earthen walls adds some "pointed" commentary to the story set-up. One reads, "Some critters ain't never gonna learn!" while the other proclaims, "You can't run away from trouble...ain't no place that far." And it's easy to get the sense that the needlepoints are directly needling *you*. While the stitchery has a moralizing tone, the statements also serve to establish a mood of danger and suspense. After all, this *is* a thrill ride.

There is also a classic mythic theme beginning to assert itself as you near the boarding zone: the tendency of heroes to ignore advice to turn around, give up the quest, and go home. As you'll soon discover, these and other more direct warnings will be repeated several times during your ride...up to and even beyond the point where they can no longer possibly be effective. In some myths (such as the story of Oedipus) the hero's disregard of all the wise advice brings about a tragic outcome. In other myths, the hero's

---

colloquial English, the terms are used interchangeably, as they are in this case study.

refusal to be deterred serves to demonstrate the character's determination and worthiness. But in Brer Rabbit's case, it will only prove his selfish, reckless nature…though unlike most other tragic heroes, he will escape his self-inflicted fate, if only by a "hare."

Though Brer Rabbit may be too obstinate to turn back, you still have one last opportunity to refuse your Call to Adventure. Just before you reach the ride's load zone, a themed chicken-out poster warns "LAST CHANCE TO EXIT." Undeterred, you press ahead and moments later you and your traveling companions are climbing aboard your eight-passenger log.

That log appears to have been carved out by a team of sharp-toothed beavers. But it is the Brer Rabbit figurehead at the front of your log that has special meaning. It's more than a rustic hood ornament; it also signifies that you will be experiencing Brer Rabbit's adventures through his eyes. Wherever he goes in and around Splash Mountain, you will go too, and his destiny in this Special World will be your own.

A moment later, your log is dispatched and you are sloshing along the channel and onto the first lift—one of many threshold crossings awaiting you on your adventure. As you ascend through a rocky tunnel, a figure appears at the edge of the waterway. It's Brer Frog again—this time "in the flesh"—and he's not shy about expressing his opinion. "If you ask me," he croaks, "sooner or later Brer Fox and Brer Bear are gonna catch that Brer Rabbit." It's a classic herald moment, and his warning that Brer Rabbit is heading down a dangerous path will be echoed by several other characters over the next few minutes.

Arriving at the top of the first lift, you begin drifting through the outer edges of the briar patch. On your right, you can see the towering summit of Chick-a-Pin Hill and catch a glimpse of your own fate as logs filled with screaming passengers hurtle down the precipitous slope, disappearing into the briar patch below and producing the mighty splashdown that gives the attraction its name. You are so close to the action, you may even catch a bit of the overspray before your log begins ascending the next lift. And though the scene is a closer version of the Call to Adventure view you received when you first approached the attraction, by now you have fully committed to your Journey. Like it or not, there's no turning back from your heroic destiny.

The second lift is enclosed within a barn-like structure, the interior of which is lined with barrels and burlap bags stacked on wooden shelves—an efficient brain script designed to remind you that you are in an inhabited realm. Then, emerging at the top of the lift, you suddenly find yourself floating through another part of the critter community as an instrumental version of the song "How Do You Do?" drifts through the air. Amidst red clay hills, a homespun "Welcome!" sign stamped with a paw print marks this latest threshold crossing. And though none of the local residents is on view to greet you, there's plenty of evidence of their ongoing presence, including a vegetable garden, a clothesline (complete with tiny shirts and trousers), and several more of those elaborate birdhouses. There's also a whisky still labeled "Muskrat Moonshine" and a medicine show wagon hawking "Critter Elixir." Nearby, three rustic wooden signs on a signpost point to "Brer Fox's Lair," "Chick-a-Pin Falls," and "The Laughing Place," fulfilling the role of the herald archetype and clueing you into three locations that will prove highly significant during your voyage.

But first, there's a major threshold fast approaching: Slippin' Falls—a short drop that deposits you inside the mountain for the interior portion of the ride. Just ahead of the cave-like portal, a beehive hangs overhead, suspended from a fallen tree trunk. Though you may not realize it yet, bees and beehives will serve a vital function later in your adventure, so this initial appearance provides a bit of foreshadowing.

As in many Disney "dark rides," the interior portion of Splash Mountain is designed to represent an outdoor environment. And so, as you enter the mountain, you find yourself passing an outdoor fishin' hole, where a gaggle of Audio-Animatronic geese is happily angling (despite a prominent "No Fishin'" sign). They are accompanied by several frogs as they sing the "How Do You Do?" song. On the opposite bank, Brer Fox and Brer bear yuck it up as they set a snare trap for Brer Rabbit, following the directions in a book they brought along titled, appropriately, *How To Catch A Rabbit*. These are, of course, the story's two antagonists— the shadow figures of your Hero's Journey—driven by their primitive instincts. After all, despite their human clothes and their ability to speak, Brer Fox and Brer Bear are, at heart, a couple of wild animals.

The story's hero, Brer Rabbit, meanwhile is driven by an impulse beyond the instinct for mere survival. Seen nearby preparing to set off from his briar patch home, he sings to his friend Mr. Bluebird: *"I'm lookin' for a little more adventure...I'm hopin' for a little more excitement."* It's a classic hero's declaration, confirming that Brer Rabbit has embraced his personal Hero's Journey and is prepared to fulfill his destiny. But is he truly ready for what awaits him? The other critters don't seem to think so. Commenting from the banks of the waterway, Mr. Porky Pine and Mr. Skunk express their skepticism, singing: *"Hey Brer Rabbit better mend your ways. You're headin' for trouble one of these days."*

Then: *"Warnin' this rabbit I'm afraid is a waste. He's makin' his way to the Laughin' Place."*

Moments later, a new scene reveals itself as you catch a glimpse of Brer Rabbit in silhouette, leading the silhouettes of Brer Fox and Brer Bear on a merry chase along a distant hilltop. In the foreground, a couple of young bunnies are doing chores around their little hillside cottage and commenting on the action. With a tone of disappointed resignation, they remark on Brer Rabbit's forthcoming rendezvous with trouble. Even at their tender age, the two bunnies clearly possess the common sense that Brer Rabbit sorely lacks. Like Mr. Porky Pine and Mr. Skunk, they too are heralds.

The next scene reveals the outcome of the chase, with Brer Bear caught in his own snare trap as Brer Fox prepares to chop him down. While simple-minded Brer Bear is dumbfounded by the unexpected reversal, Brer Fox is livid. He complains bitterly that Brer Rabbit is making them look like fools. For Brer Fox at least, the pursuit is now a personal vendetta. Brer Rabbit only deepens the antagonism as he hops away, taunting "You boys can't catch me!" and declaring that he's off to find the Laughing Place. The stakes are mounting and Brer Fox literally has an ax to grind.

The route to the Laughing Place is populated by a Greek chorus of woodland critters including frogs, an alligator, a roadrunner, and a trio of opossums, all cheerfully singing "Everybody's Got a Laughing Place." The upbeat song belies the true menace of the place, which will soon become abundantly obvious—though too late to prevent Brer Rabbit from an all-too-close encounter with his own mortality.

In fact, the Laughing Place turns out to be the first of several Inmost Caves and Supreme Ordeals that Brer Rabbit will have to endure (as will you and your log-mates, since you're all irrevocably committed to his Journey). And, as fate would have it, the Inmost Cave known as the Laughing Place takes the form of a literal cave. At the entrance, you'll notice Brer Fox and Brer Bear have already arrived on the scene. Not being the sharpest knives in the drawer, Brer Fox is trying to push Brer Bear through a too-small opening in the cave wall as Brer Rabbit secretly watches with great amusement from another opening. Of course, Brer Bear reports there's no trace of Brer Rabbit. However, he does notice that the cave is filled with bees.

Fortunately, your log finds a much more accommodating entrance into the cave involving a brief "dip-drop" through darkness. Emerging in the first chamber, you find a cavern swarming with bees circling several beehives scattered around the space. Since you left the previous scene, Brer Bear has evidently tumbled through the opening into this cavern and now one of the beehives is firmly lodged on his nose. He writhes in agony as the bees attack him, while Brer Rabbit literally rolls on the ground, convulsed with laughter at the sight of his adversary's predicament. In fact, he's so busy laughing, he fails to notice that Brer Fox has snuck up behind him and is preparing to clobber him with another beehive. The danger is so imminent, you can hardly "bear" to watch.

Fortunately, another short drop lands your log in a second cavern and you find you have arrived in Brer Rabbit's long-sought Laughing Place. Here, turtles and other critters play and sing amidst a phosphorescent sprayground of geysers and leaping waters. Yet the Laughing Place turns out to be a fool's paradise as Brer Rabbit discovers that the "honey and rainbows" promised by the song lyrics come at a terrible price. But it's not like he wasn't warned. The "How Do You Do?" song heard earlier includes the repeated line, "Time to be turnin' around." And now you drift past wooden signs inside the Laughing Place warning "Danger" and "Go back!" Unfortunately, Brer Rabbit has long since passed the point of no return, and the next time you see him, he is bound up inside a beehive against a menacing backdrop of stalactites and stalagmites. Brer Fox grips him firmly by the ears, declaring, "You're mine, you're mine! And you ain't gettin' away this time!" while Brer Rabbit pleads piteously to be set free.

Now you enter a third Inmost Cave: a steep lift hill through a darkened tunnel. Two vultures dressed like undertakers are perched over the tunnel entrance, functioning as threshold guardians. "If you finally found your Laughing Place...how come you aren't laughing?" they ask in a taunting tone. Meanwhile, the music has taken a sharply dramatic turn, building in its intensity as your log makes its slow but inevitable ascent.

Near the top, you come upon Brer Fox's lair where Brer Rabbit is roped to a stake alongside a giant cooking pot. Brer Fox (a literal shadow figure at this point) can be heard trying to decide whether to hang or roast his captive. Brer Rabbit tells him to "Go ahead...but don't fling me in that briar patch!" This is his Supreme Ordeal...and yours, too. Yet there's one more Inmost Cave to endure: the monstrous, mist-shrouded briar patch that yawns menacingly at the bottom of the drop, 52 feet below you.

Before you can brace yourself, gravity takes hold and your log is sent plummeting at 40 miles-per-hour into the heart of the briar patch, resulting in a huge, drenching splashdown. Seconds later, you emerge from the briars, half-soaked but otherwise no worse for wear, and laughing with a combination of relief and excitement. You have survived your final Supreme Ordeal and now you and Brer Rabbit are homeward bound.

As it happens, one more cave awaits you during the Return movement of your Journey—this one the domain of a joyous welcoming committee. "WELCOME HOME BRER RABBIT" reads the handmade banner suspended over the threshold. Inside, you glide past a showboat crowded with jubilant critters belting out an especially buoyant rendition of the song "Zip-a-dee-doo-dah." Around the corner, you find that Brer Fox and Brer Bear have not given up the fight, having followed Brer Rabbit into the briars. But now the predators have become the prey as a hungry gator has clamped its jaws onto Brer Fox's tail.

Finally, you come upon Brer Rabbit, home at last and singing, *"I'm through with movin' on now."* It turns out Brer Rabbit was "born and bred" in the briar patch and was quite happy to have Brer Fox return him to his family abode. As Mr. Bluebird listens, Brer Rabbit continues: *"Zip-a-dee-doo-dah, zip-a-dee-ay, I'm back in my home now and I'm sure gonna' stay."* But if Mr. Bluebird looks a little skeptical, he has every reason to be, considering Brer Rabbit's personal history. As the framed needlepoint mounted in the exit corridor observes, "If'n Brer Rabbit ain't changed his ways, he'll meet up with more troubles one of these days!"

The last thing you see from your log before you arrive at the load/unload platform is a large graphic painted across two walls declaring, "It's the truth, it's actual...Everything is satisfactual." But the "truth" is, none of it is "actual." The entire ride and the Uncle Remus stories it was loosely based on were all made up. Yet at the same time, like all myths, your Splash Mountain Journey was totally truthful—from a psychological perspective, that is. Brer Rabbit's adventurous impulses are very similar to our own. And his stubborn insistence on pursuing his passions, despite numerous warnings of danger ahead, also reflects a very human trait.

Splash Mountain, as we have seen, is loaded with symbolic imagery. One of the most intriguing is the prominent and recurrent presence of bees and beehives at key points in the show. While they obviously serve a basic narrative function as the ride's storyline unfolds, their significance goes much deeper. Which is not surprising when you consider the mythic roles they have played over millennia. For example, bees were sacred to the ancient Egyptians, who associated them with the sun god Râ. In France, the bee was revered as a symbol of Imperial rule, with Napoleon using the bee as a motif on carpets and coronation robes. They also symbolize industriousness and teamwork—qualities that contrast with Brer Rabbit's self-centered independence and his relentless pursuit of excitement in seeking out the Laughing Place.

In some early cultures, the bee was considered a link between the natural world and the underworld. In parts of ancient Greece, tombs were even shaped like beehives. Thus, it hardly seems like a coincidence that the bees in Splash Mountain are all found in the subterranean realm of the Laughing Place. Also in Greek mythology, bees are sometimes associated with the gift of prophecy—though one needn't be a prophet to foretell that Brer Rabbit is heading for trouble, as many of his neighbor critters have already figured out on their own. The ancient Greeks also believed that honey was the nectar of the gods and thus a symbol of knowledge, learning, and wisdom. Following his adventure amongst the bees of the Laughing Place, Brer Rabbit at least claims to have learned his lesson—though whether he will retain that lesson or revert to his former ways remains an open question.

Similarly, to psychoanalysts and mythologists, honey is considered a symbol of one's higher self. In the beehive, honeybees naturally transform pollen—an inedible and relatively perishable substance—into tasty, wholesome honey capable of being stored for consumption almost indefinitely. In the same way, the initiatory experience of the Hero's Journey, with its movements of Separation, Descent, Ordeal, and Return, results in the metamorphosis of the hero into a mature, fully integrated individual. That, of course, is the whole point of the Hero's Journey.

By the end of his Splash Mountain adventure, it seems Brer Rabbit has also discovered his higher self, declaring that he's learned his lesson and will be staying put from now on. But as the exit signage indicates, and as you may already suspect, it likely won't be long before he is once again seduced by the Call of Adventure.

Mania Happy Returns
Toy Story Midway Mania!

AT FIRST GLANCE, TOY STORY MIDWAY MANIA! might not appear especially mythic. "It's a ride through a virtual shooting gallery," you may be saying to yourself. "Where's the mythic content in that?" Good point, dear reader. On the other hand, the goal of this book is to reveal the mythic source code that's "hidden in plain sight" throughout the Disney theme parks, with a focus on a semi-representative cross-section of some of Disney's most popular attractions. And, as we shall soon discover, the mythic content in Toy Story Mania![28] is a lot less hidden than you might suppose.

You'll find similar iterations of Toy Story Mania! at Disney California Adventure, Tokyo DisneySea, and Disney's Hollywood Studios. The ride portions of all three experiences are virtually identical, while the façades and queues each have their own unique design direction and character. For the purposes of this attraction case study, we will limit our mythic analysis to the version at Disney's Hollywood Studios.

The first giveaway that you are about to embark on a classic Campbellian Hero's Journey hits you almost immediately as you encounter the attraction's elaborately detailed entrance. The gateway has a deliberately improvised appearance, composed of super-sized Tinker Toys, letter blocks, Scrabble tiles, crayons, playing cards, and other toys and game pieces — the handiwork, evidently,

---

[28] The entry marquee calls the attraction "Toy Story Midway Mania!" but all the advertising and promotional materials — including Disney's own website — call it "Toy Story Mania!" And therefore, so shall I.

of the *Toy Story* movies' ever-resourceful Green Army Men, some of whom are also on view.

The gateway form is a classic threshold marker—the dividing line between the Ordinary World (in this case, the park's Pixar Place section), and the Special World of the Toy Story Mania! queue. The Green Army Men and the oversized game pieces and toys, meanwhile, serve as archetypal heralds, alerting you to the wonders awaiting you just beyond the threshold.

Often in the Hero's Journey, upon entering the Special World, the hero finds that "the rules are different here." This is emphatically the case as you enter the Toy Story Mania! queue[29] and begin switchbacking through "Andy's room," where you discover you have been reduced to the size of one of Andy's toys. The sudden change in scale requires no verbal explanation; the operative brain script ("You are now a toy") is clear, straightforward, and unmistakable, thanks in part to your familiarity with the *Toy Story* movies. Ginormous versions of familiar childhood toys and games are scattered everywhere (Andy apparently hasn't cleaned up his room in quite a while)—all of them impressively detailed. Who knew your heroic Journey would turn out to be a nostalgia trip?

Beyond the giant props, the bedroom wallpaper perfectly matches the art direction from the first *Toy Story* movie. Other direct references to the movies are also worked into the scenery in ways that are sometimes subtle, and sometimes explicit. In the latter category is the Mr. Potato Head "Boardwalk Barker" toy—a five-foot-tall Audio-Animatronic figure with the voice of Don Rickles. The scaled-up cardboard carton in which Mr. Potato Head supposedly came packaged is also on view, its graphics

---

[29] This case study describes the guest experience from the viewpoint of the standby queue.

revealing that the anthropomorphic spud is a part of the Midway Mania! play set ("sold separately.") Batteries not included.

The talkative tuber here assumes the role of the mythic herald...and does so quite enthusiastically, inviting prospective midway players to "Step right up!" Often in mythology, it is the herald's job to announce the Call to Adventure. At Toy Story Mania!, this task has already been fulfilled by the heavily themed entry gate and marquee. Now Mr. Potato Head reinforces that Call with his own barker-style patter, and offers a verbal preview of some of the challenges you'll be facing during your adventure (another heraldic function).

Those ingenious Imagineers have also equipped Mr. Potato Head with the ability to banter directly with guests using a recording of Mr. Rickles' distinctive voice. The character even makes seemingly spontaneous references to, and wisecracks about, the appearance of specific guests as they pass within teasing range. It's all a clever technological trick, of course...but a very effective one. Which may or may not make Mr. Potato Head both a herald archetype and a trickster. Or maybe it's those crafty Imagineers who are the actual tricksters.

As the mythic hero travels through the unfamiliar landscape of the Special World, she is likely to encounter a mentor or other allies who may equip her with magical weapons, tools, vehicles, amulets, talismans, or other objects necessary for the quest. In the classical Greek myth, the hero Perseus receives Hades' helmet of invisibility, Hermes' adamantine sword, and a polished shield from Athena, so that he can defeat the snake-haired monster known as Medusa. So what do *you* get? How about a pair of plastic 3-D glasses? Yet those flimsy-looking glasses serve an essential mythic function. For when you slip on these enchanted spectacles at the appropriate point in your Journey, stereoscopic images that would appear meaningless (or at least annoying) to your unaided eyes will miraculously become endowed with purpose and value.

Soon, your Journey delivers you to another threshold: the Approach to the Inmost Cave, where your chariot—the eight-passenger Toy Story Mania! vehicle—awaits. The vehicle is another "magical gift" from your yet-to-be-seen mentors, with each passenger seat equipped with a colorful "spring-action shooter." As you'll soon discover, this remarkable cannon-shaped device is capable of firing an amazing assortment of virtual projectiles—from chicken eggs and baseballs to darts and rings. The shooter will fire as often as you can pull the string. And best of all, it never runs out of ammo.

Often in the structure of a Hero's Journey narrative, the crossing into the Inmost Cave—the site of the Supreme Ordeal—is preceded by an interval of tests, training, and preparations, which the mythologist Joseph Campbell referred to as "the Road of Trials." In Toy Story Mania!, however, the Road of Trials and the Inmost Cave are combined. Thus, moments after you are secured in your ride vehicle, you are swept into the UV-illuminated 3-D environment of the Toy Story midway where you will encounter a series of heroic tests.

As we learned earlier, tests and trials are fundamental elements of the Hero's Journey, for it is during this stage of the adventure that the hero sharpens the skills that will be needed in order to complete the quest. In the Roman myth of Cupid and Psyche, for example, poor love-struck Psyche must accomplish one impossibly cruel task after another assigned to her by Cupid's vindictive mother Venus. First she has to sort a mountain of mixed seeds...then she must collect the golden wool of a particularly nasty man-eating sheep (yes—*a man-eating sheep*)...then steal a bottle of water guarded by a fearsome dragon...and finally she must descend to the underworld, overcome the monstrous three-headed guard dog Cerberus, and retrieve "a box full of supernatural beauty." And all this happens *before* Psyche faces her Supreme Ordeal later in the tale.

Fortunately, the tests awaiting you are a lot more enjoyable. They chiefly involve using your spring-action shooter to hit an assortment of animated shooting gallery-style targets presented on a series of large 3-D video screens as you attempt to drive your personal score as high as you can. And like winsome Psyche, you are aided by allies and mentors—at least initially. In Toy Story Mania!, your mentors take the form of the core characters from the Toy Story movies: Sheriff Woody, Buzz Lightyear, and Cowgirl Jessie. Appearing at the first game booth, they guide you through a quick "practice round," hoisting circular target shields and shouting encouragement as you send dozens of pies flying toward them.

Rolling onward to the next booth, it's time for the first of the "real" games: "Hamm & Eggs" (an egg throw game). This is followed by "Rex and Trixie's Dino Darts" (a dart throw game, previously "Bo Peep's Baaa-loon Pop"), "Green Army Men Shoot Camp" (a baseball throw/plate breaking game), "Buzz Lightyear's Flying Tossers" (a ring toss game), and finally "Woody's Rootin' Tootin' Shootin' Gallery" (a suction cup shooting game).

Is this final booth the one for which the preceding booths have been preparing you? Does this make the "Shootin' Gallery" booth the Supreme Ordeal? Or were all the challenges merely intended to prepare you for another unspecified Supreme Ordeal somewhere beyond this attraction? Does it really matter? In a word: *No.* Not in the slightest. For by the time you have noted your score and exited your ride vehicle, Toy Story Mania! has fulfilled its mythic function. Though you probably won't feel as though you've died and been resurrected as you return to the Ordinary World of the park's Pixar Place section, you will surely feel energized and uplifted. Thus, for a few minutes at least, you will have undergone a personal transformation. And that is the essence of the Hero's Journey.

Life in the Fast Lane
Test Track Presented by Chevrolet

IT'S NATURAL TO THINK OF FUTURE WORLD as the Epcot equivalent of Tomorrowland. In their original incarnations, the Tomorrowlands of Disneyland and Walt Disney World's Magic Kingdom were direct expressions of Walt Disney's optimistic vision of the future. The same can be said of Future World. Unfortunately, like its Tomorrowland cousins, Future World continuously transforms into "Present Day World" as scientific and technological advances catch up to, and sometimes even surpass, the once-visionary attractions. All too soon, what was originally considered revolutionary and cutting-edge starts to seem commonplace or even quaint.

The Disney Imagineers eventually made a creative end-run around the problem of keeping the "tomorrow" in Tomorrowland. At Disneyland and in the Magic Kingdom, they re-imagined the land as an intergalactic spaceport, with nostalgic, retro-futuristic theming inspired by early 20th century concepts of the things to come. Hong Kong Disneyland's Tomorrowland opened with a similar "spaceport" theme already in place. And Disneyland Paris' version of Tomorrowland, known as "Discoveryland," has also relied on the retro-futuristic approach all along, though its thematic direction takes its cues from the imaginations of Victorian-era science fiction writers Jules Verne and H.G. Wells.[30] By adopting this "futures past" direction, the Imagineers assured that Tomorrowland would always possess the same timeless quality as the parks' other lands.

---

[30] Tokyo Disneyland's version of Tomorrowland, on the other hand, still largely resembles its Orlando counterpart, circa 1975.

No such re-theming option exists at fact-based Epcot, where Future World's attractions must be "refreshed" every so often or risk becoming laughably outdated. That's why every current attraction in Future World has undergone at least one significant overhaul over the years. In at least two cases, the attractions have gone away entirely: Horizons was completely demolished to make way for Mission: SPACE, while the golden dome that once housed Wonders of Life was divested of its attractions, becoming an all-purpose special events venue.

Though the cavernous, silver-skinned cylinder that now serves as the home of Test Track Presented by Chevrolet is the same iconic structure that has stood on the site since Epcot (then known as "EPCOT Center") first opened its gates in October 1982, the experience inside has twice undergone some of the most dramatic changes of any attraction in Future World. Yet in every iteration, the mythic energy of the Hero's Journey has always resonated strongly, contributing to the popularity of all three occupants of the venue.

The first of those occupants was World of Motion Presented by General Motors. The theme—and theme song—was "It's fun to be free," which set the upbeat tone for a whimsical, slow-moving jaunt through the history of transportation, from primitive foot-power to futuristic mass transit systems. Most of the mythic Journey was concentrated on the Road of Trials stage (experienced in the ride as a literal road) with frequent embedded threshold crossings as Guests skipped from one historical era to the next, encountering new transportation developments with each transition. Eventually, their Journey led them to the Inmost Cave—a "speed tunnel" sequence in which projected point-of-view action footage was combined with wind effects and the motion of the Omnimover ride vehicle to impart a semi-effective sensation of tremendous acceleration.

In 1999, the time-travel storyline was replaced by an entirely new transportation-based theme as World of Motion became GM Test Track and the leisurely excursion through transportation history was supplanted by "the thrill of safety-testing a prototype vehicle on a variable speed, multi-surface, multi-environment testing course." The all-new experience featured a Road of Trials that was composed of a series of harrowing safety tests, including an Inmost Cave encounter that involved a near-collision with a semi tractor-trailer inside a cave-like tunnel, and a high-speed Return sequence along an outdoor raceway.

In late 2012, GM Test Track was "reimagined" as Test Track Presented by Chevrolet, with the focus on auto safety testing giving way to a storyline centered on the art and technology of automotive design. While the thrills and dynamism remain the same and the ride vehicles reflect only cosmetic changes, the new show narrative, along with every aspect of the thematic design, creates a completely new experience—one that taps directly into the modern myths of cyberspace and telecommunications.

Your Test Track 2.0[31] Journey begins as you enter Test Track Plaza in Future World East, where you get a preliminary glimpse of the design-centered experience awaiting you inside the great wheel-shaped show building. Your first hint of this stylish Special World is the aerodynamic blue "speed form" sculpture mounted above the attraction marquee. The gleaming sculpture, as you will soon learn, represents an idealized automotive shape and is

---

[31] The current attraction's official title is "Test Track Presented by Chevrolet," but it is often referred to casually as "Test Track 2.0" or just plain old "Test Track." For simplicity's sake, the remainder of this case study will use all three names interchangeably.

similar to speed forms created by professional automotive designers as they envision tomorrow's vehicles. Though you may not realize it yet, speed forms like this one will play a foundational role during your Test Track adventure.

The speed form's abstract-looking shape also offers another clue about what's to come, with its subtly curved or "bowed" lines soon to be echoed in the architecture, scenic design, graphics, display media, and throughout the Guest-interactive portions of the pre-show experience. You can already discern it in the design of the graphic banners suspended around the plaza. In this sense, the marquee sculpture is very much a mythic herald, announcing that the first stage of your Hero's Journey is fast approaching, if not already underway.

In Test Track Plaza, you are also exposed for the first time to the attraction's inspirational background music score—an upbeat, minimalist composition that's as clean and streamlined as the marquee speed form. The music is frequently punctuated by the roar of the "Sim Car" ride vehicles as they zoom overhead at white-knuckle speeds, one after another, along a portion of the exterior "Turbo Track." It's a pulse-quickening preview of the Return movement of your forthcoming Journey. But first, you have a major threshold to cross as you accept your Call to Adventure and enter the Special World of the attraction's pre-show experience.[32]

Passing through the building entrance, you find yourself transported to the sleekly modernistic setting of a contemporary automotive design facility. Here, you can see the bowed line of the marquee sculpture expressed throughout the space's interior design—in the rounded

---

[32] Since the FASTPASS/Individual Rider pre-show experience on Test Track is highly abbreviated, this case study describes only the standby guest experience.

walls and ceiling treatment, in the graceful swoop of the wing wall, and in the softly angled portals and frames. The room's evocative lighting draws your attention to the several full-size concept vehicles that populate the facility, along with a number of vehicle models, speed forms, and video displays. Meanwhile, the stylishly minimalistic background music continues, taking on a slightly different character from area to area to complement the displays in each zone. Combined, these elements present a "world of tomorrow" brain script that's very much in sync with the attraction's Future World East setting.

This space is your introduction to the Special World of automotive design — an actual profession that you and many of your fellow adventurers may never have given any thought to until now. You may feel like a stranger in a strange land, surrounded by esoteric imagery and ideas that have little connection to your daily life in the Ordinary World. But that's the essential purpose of the mythic Special World: to take the hero out of his element, prodding him to learn "the lay of the land" in a new and unfamiliar setting, and begin to explore his own capabilities in the process.

Studying the pre-show models, videos, concept cars, and graphics, no one could blame you for feeling somewhat overwhelmed — and possibly even a bit intimidated — by the highly technical nature of the displays. Yet despite your possible misgivings, like any true hero you press ahead with your Journey. Soon enough, your perseverance is rewarded as you begin to recognize a pattern emerging in your surroundings. Specifically, you notice an emphasis on the idea of "Performance Attributes," along with the recurrence of the words "Capability," "Efficiency," "Responsiveness," and "Power." It becomes increasingly clear that these terms have significance in this Special World, and will no doubt play an important role later in your adventure.

Congratulations! By simply moving forward through the pre-show queue, observing and absorbing your surroundings along the way (rather than abandoning your Journey, thank you very much), you have proven yourself worthy of crossing the next threshold. That transition takes you into a rotunda-like chamber featuring a "blank" speed form on a pedestal. Behind the model, a wall-mounted media screen features a montage of individuals, young and old, who take turns describing the cars of their dreams. Interspersed among these brief monologues are equally brief vignettes of auto designers speaking candidly and enthusiastically about their professions. As they speak, the blank speed form becomes a projection surface onto which are mapped a succession of images illustrating the on-screen comments.

The presentation is not just engaging; it also casts the subject of automotive design in a whole new context, humanizing it and making this relatively technical topic suddenly accessible. At this point, it may dawn on you that the automobile designers in this presentation are not so different from you and your fellow adventurers. Yes, they bring certain specialized skills to their profession. But more than anything else, it is their passion—their love of great design and their enthusiasm for all things automotive—that propels them in their individual creative Journeys. They are the heroes who have gone before you, blazing a trail in this Special World, and their personal stories now serve as a catalyst and inspiration for your own Journey.

Though it may be far from obvious at first, every part of your trek through the queue thus far has been in preparation for the Supreme Ordeal that awaits you a few moments from now within the Inmost Cave. Those preparations have largely dealt with acclimating you to the rarefied realm in which expert automotive designers dwell.

Up to this point, the familiarization process has been a strictly hands-off experience. But now that's about to change as you enter a section of the queue, where your experience becomes hands-on in the most literal sense.

Pausing at one of the four large, wall-mounted touchscreen displays, you follow a set of simple on-screen prompts as you practice drawing a gestural line and then watch as your line defines the profile of an automotive speed form. You can then manipulate various grab points along your profile line to change the shape of the virtual speed form. As you shape and re-shape the onscreen speed form, you can see how each change affects the four Performance Attributes.

Yes, as you had earlier suspected, those Attributes— "Capability," "Efficiency," "Responsiveness," and "Power"—have come into play...and not for the last time, either. Though your training here is brief, the new skills you develop in the process will prove vital as you begin your Supreme Ordeal. But first, a few words from your mentor.

Often in the structure of the mythic Hero's Journey, the Meeting with the Mentor occurs early in the adventure— sometimes even before the Crossing of the First Threshold. But in Test Track 2.0, your first encounter with your mentor takes place in the lobby outside the Chevrolet Design Studio—the Inmost Cave of your Journey. During his Approach to the Inmost Cave, the hero may be aided by one or more allies. Your mythic ally in this lobby space is a friendly Test Track cast member, who presents you with a magical talisman: a "Design Key" card that will unlock the power of the touchscreen Design Station kiosk for you as you are challenged to design your own virtual Chevrolet Custom Concept Vehicle.[33] Yes, as you may have already begun to suspect, your aptitude as an automotive designer

---

[33] If you have a MagicBand wristband, that will do the trick, too.

is about to be put to the test. The specifics of the task ahead are explained by the soothing, disembodied voice of your mentor, accompanied by the helpful graphic animation that plays across a set of media displays mounted above the automatic doors leading into the two identical Design Studios.

The interior of the Chevrolet Design Studio is about as sleek and stylish as any Inmost Cave could hope to be. The chamber is bathed in cool, blue light, while the touchscreen panels on the banks of the Design Station kiosks radiate a beckoning glow. Drawing on the sage advice of your mentor moments earlier, you locate your assigned kiosk and touch your Design Key to the kiosk's card reader. The machine responds approvingly, having judged you worthy enough to face the Supreme Ordeal.

As Supreme Ordeals go, this one proves to be a lot more fun than arduous. Thanks to your interactive practice session a few moments earlier, you find you have already mastered one of the initial tasks: drawing the gestural line that will define the profile of your Custom Concept Vehicle. But then, as the base speed form materializes onscreen, you are faced with a cascade of creative decisions involving everything from the width of your vehicle to the number of wheels to the color of the body paint. And, once again, those four Performance Attributes come into play, with many of the design choices you make directly affecting your vehicle's Capability, Efficiency, Responsiveness, and Power scores. Every choice involves a trade-off of some kind: increase the Power score and you may lower your Efficiency score; increase the Responsiveness and you may adversely affect the vehicle's Capability. Finding a happy medium is no easy task, and even then the result may be a design that is not very aesthetically pleasing. Pretty soon you are developing a healthy respect for those who design automobiles for a living.

With time running out, you finalize your Custom Concept Vehicle design as your compatriots around you do the same. In the brief interval before the exit doors open, you may want to pause and appreciate what has just occurred. For in the span of a few minutes, you and your fellow adventurers have successfully completed the Supreme Ordeal. Moreover, when you leave the Inmost Cave, you will no longer be an oblivious neophyte in the Special World of automotive design. The Custom Concept Vehicle that is now associated with your Design Key provides unequivocal proof that you are emerging from the Chevrolet Design Studio as a full-fledged and highly capable automotive designer.

There's no question that your Custom Concept Vehicle looks terrific. But just how awesome is your design, really? That's where the next portion of your Journey comes into play. For in a few moments, you will be boarding a Sim Car and putting your design to the test on the Sim Track. As it happens, the digital matrix of the Sim Track is actually a second Inmost Cave, and each Performance proving course within this Cave will challenge you (or at least your Custom Concept Car design) with a new Supreme Ordeal.

As Test Track 2.0 amply demonstrates, there's no rule specifying how many Inmost Caves and Supreme Ordeals can be contained in a single Hero's Journey. Ultimately, the number and sequence of the stages in any particular Journey are determined by the needs of the hero. And so, as you arrive on the Sim Car load platform, you touch your Design Key to a designated card reader and confirm that your Custom Concept Vehicle design will be accompanying you, virtually, over the next threshold and into the Inmost Cave of the Sim Track.

As your Sim Car conveys you away from the load platform, you encounter what may very well be one of the most distinctive and dramatic threshold crossings in any Disney theme park. The luminescent, high-tech archway signals a transition into a Special World within a Special World—a wondrous, neon-like electronic themescape of circuit boards and graphic patterns that appears to "rez-up" around you as you ascend the lift hill. But the threshold is only one of several within this digital Inmost Cave, for each Performance proving course along the Sim Track is accompanied by its own glowing, ring-shaped portal, along with a Performance Display monitor that compares your Custom Concept Vehicle's performance to those of your fellow travelers (and to the performance of the Sim Car in which you are all riding).

The first of these four portals—this one belonging to the Capability proving course—awaits you at the top of the hill. Passing through the yellow gateway, you plunge into a punishing setting of digital snow, ice, rain, and lightning—elements calculated to reveal how well your Custom Concept Vehicle can handle challenging weather and off-road conditions. Next, a glowing green portal marks the threshold of yet another Inmost Cave as you enter the environmental testing chambers of the Efficiency proving course where your Sim Car is scanned to measure your Custom Concept Vehicle's "enviro impact."

Emerging from the Enviro Impact Chambers, you pass through a blue portal and are immediately injected onto the Responsiveness proving course for a harrowing test of your Custom Concept Vehicle's steering abilities. Accelerating as it goes, your Sim Car weaves up a switchback mountain road lined with glowing digital trees, boulders, and warning signs before entering an electronic tunnel (yet *another* Inmost Cave), narrowly avoiding a collision with a laser-rimmed tractor-trailer lurking inside. But as you catch your breath, you realize that one final challenge remains: the Power proving course. Your Sim Car rolls to a momentary stop as it energizes its propulsion system. Directly ahead of you, the purple Power portal begins to glow and pulsate—and suddenly you are hurtling toward a set of doors that snap open at the very last second to admit you to the outdoor Turbo Track. Rocketing along the course at white-knuckle speeds, you leave the digital Inmost Cave of the Sim Track behind to commence the Return movement of your Journey.

At last, your Sim Car pulls to a stop alongside the unload platform. You and your Custom Concept Vehicle have endured multiple Supreme Ordeals inside the Sim Track, proving that you have what it takes to be a hero—at least within the framework of this particular Special World. Yet after you disembark from the ride vehicle, you find that the Return portion of your adventure has only just begun. Fortunately, the road back to the Ordinary World of Future World East is lined with several entertainingly high-tech opportunities to explore the capabilities of your Custom Concept Vehicle, which exists as a virtual memento of your adventures in the Special World.

Now, in Test Track's Design Showcase (the attraction's post-show area), you can use your Design Key to review your Custom Concept Vehicle's final Performance Attribute score and compare it to those of your fellow adventurers. Nearby, you'll find Design in Motion, a large rotunda space equipped with interactive kiosks. Here, using your Design Key, you can summon your Custom Concept Vehicle from cyberspace and cast it as the star of a custom 15-second video commercial, complete with music and voiceover narration.

If you are feeling competitive, you can challenge your fellow adventurers to a virtual road race at any of Design

Showcase's three Give it a Spin! stations. Just sidle up to an available console, each of which is equipped with a steering wheel, a throttle arm, and a card reader. Again, your Design Key is your ticket to ride, with your Custom Concept Vehicle zooming around the augmented reality racetrack alongside the virtual vehicles of your opponents. Elsewhere, you can pose for a souvenir photo with a computer-simulated rendering of your Custom Concept Vehicle or an actual Chevrolet car or truck. Finally, you can browse the Test Track logo merchandise and other souvenirs of your Journey in the After Market Shop in pursuit of a physical token of your adventures.

Altogether, the current incarnation of Test Track is not so much about transportation as it is about *transformation* — the hallmark of every mythic Hero's Journey. The transformative theme is experienced on several levels. First, there's the transformation that you witnessed as you evolved a gestural line into a speed form and ultimately into a complete Custom Concept Vehicle ready to be tested on the Sim Track. Then there's the personal transformation you experienced as you morphed from an outsider and novice into an up-and-coming designer with the skill and insight required to create your own Custom Concept Vehicle.[34]

Test Track 2.0 reminds us that the role of the hero exists on different levels. It's not always about mortal self-sacrifice. There are other kinds of service that a hero can provide for the benefit of the community. Indeed, like motor vehicles, heroes come in all makes and models. But the first requirement of every hero is a commitment to the quest—

---

[34] A third, more historical series of transformations may be appreciated by longtime Epcot fans: the evolution from the pavilion's original incarnation as World of Motion into GM Test Track and then, ultimately, into Test Track Presented by Chevrolet.

the willingness to accept the Call to Adventure and embrace one's destiny.

Mythologist Joseph Campbell's oft-quoted advice to "Follow your bliss" is beautifully embodied in the pre-show testimonies of the on-screen automotive designers, whose boundless enthusiasm for their profession is unmistakable. For these individuals, the joy of seeing their designs realized as actual, functional vehicles is nearly transcendent. It is closely related to the spontaneous expressions of delight frequently heard at the Design Station kiosks as Test Track guests finalize their Custom Concept Vehicles.

For the community at large, the auto designers' creativity can result in better vehicles, better transportation systems, and ultimately better communities—an idea specifically conveyed in the pre-show's EN-V/Technology & Innovation display. Here, the attraction's storyline turns its focus to the problems confronting the world's burgeoning megacities, and the role automotive designers are playing in addressing these urgent issues. The two full-size EN-V [35] models, accompanied by a video loop showing the vehicles in action, demonstrate how these unusual-looking vehicles may someday help to reduce traffic congestion and energy consumption while providing better parking and safety, and improving the quality of city life overall.

This is just one more way in which Test Track Presented by Chevrolet epitomizes the spirit of invention that informs every Future World attraction. It is also an exemplary demonstration of Walt Disney's original vision of the city of EPCOT—his "Experimental Prototype Community of Tomorrow"—that would serve as "...a living showcase for American free enterprise at its most creative and forward-looking." It was a soaring vision—one that defined Walt's

---

[35] Electric Networked-Vehicles

own Hero's Journey in the latter years of his remarkable life and career.

Tomb it May Concern
Haunted Mansion

MANY DISNEY ATTRACTIONS DELIVER THEIR THRILLS by pretending to put you in peril—either personally (as in Indiana Jones Adventure and Big Thunder Mountain) or vicariously (Pinocchio's Daring Journey, Snow White's Scary Adventures). But the Haunted Mansion is one of the few that purport to send you into the afterlife...or at least offer you a peek into the Great Beyond. Unless you count the "white room" scene near the end of "it's a small world" (which some guests reportedly assume represents some sort of international "singing doll heaven,") the remainder of the attractions list is pretty much limited to the finale scene of Mr. Toad's Wild Ride and the various iterations of Tower of Terror.

The Haunted Mansion's ubiquity in the Magic Kingdom-class parks around the world testifies to the attraction's inherent appeal. Each version is unique in its own ways, with some differences more significant than others. In Disneyland Paris, for example, where the attraction is known as Phantom Manor, the sequence of scenes is notably different from its counterparts in the U.S. and Japan, as is the storyline's emphasis (though the overall theme remains largely intact).[36] Only Hong Kong Disneyland, among the Magic Kingdom-class parks, is devoid of a version of the Haunted Mansion.[37] For the

---

[36] The differences between the various Haunted Mansion attractions are spelled out in detail by Imagineer Jason Surrell in his book *The Haunted Mansion: From the Magic Kingdom to the Movies* (Disney Editions, 2003)
[37] Out of cultural considerations involving traditional Chinese sensitivities toward the subject of ghosts, that niche in the park's

purposes of this case study, however, we'll focus solely on the Magic Kingdom rendition.

Your first good view of the Haunted Mansion will typically be from the quaint colonial environs of Liberty Square—a Special World within the Special World of the Magic Kingdom. In the same way, Liberty Square represents the Ordinary World relative to the Special World of the Haunted Mansion. The Dutch-Gothic style manor house looms over Liberty Square—a foreboding presence atop a low hill, set apart from the other attractions yet impossible to ignore...especially with the frequent wolf howls serving as a chilling Call to Adventure that can be heard throughout the area and even from Tom Sawyer Island.

Of course no one can resist the enchanting strains of a nice, full-throated wolf howl. And so, accepting the Call, you follow your ears through the wrought-iron gate and onto the manor's grounds. Traversing the neatly manicured entry drive, you pass a glossy black horse-drawn hearse, which appears to be hitched up to an invisible horse, the contours of its body discernable only by the shapes of its leather harness. Though you have barely crossed the First Threshold into the Special World of the Haunted Mansion, already you are finding that the rules are different here.

Soon, the queue leads you into the family cemetery, where the graves of various loved ones feature headstones playfully hinting at their less-than-virtuous lives and their not-so-dignified demises. But there's something else that sets this cemetery apart from those of the Ordinary World. For here, the dearly departed refuse to entirely depart. Instead, several of them linger in our mortal realm well past their expiration dates—in spirit, at least—and are fond of

---

attraction portfolio is occupied by Mystic Manor, a dark ride that immerses its guests in an all-new supernatural adventure.

making their presences known in whimsically macabre ways. Thus, the pipe organ-shaped tomb of a decomposing composer plays his favorite tune ("Grim Grinning Ghosts") when you touch the sculpted stone keyboard, while the sepulcher of "Captain Culpepper Clyne," (who was "allergic to dirt so he's pickled in brine") douses nearby mourners with a spritz of saltwater whenever its occupant sneezes. And so it appears that, by entering the domain of the dead, you are already beginning to display a nascent ability to interact with them.

Arriving at the Mansion's imposing front door, you are soon greeted by a lugubrious-looking servant, who dolefully bids you enter. This time your threshold crossing is a literal one, and it delivers you into a gloomy foyer, where a portrait of a dashing young man quickly ages—"Dorian Gray" style—until the subject is reduced to a putrefying corpse. This, it turns out, will be just one of many transformations you'll be encountering in the course of your Journey. Meanwhile, speaking over the sound of a mournful organ arrangement of "Grim Grinning Ghosts," the disembodied voice of the Ghost Host welcomes you and the other "foolish mortals" in your group. He then issues the Haunted Mansion's first official Call to Adventure as he invites you to step into the Portrait Gallery. It seems that, simply by being here, you've already accepted the Call. For as your Ghost Host informs you with an audible smirk, "There's no turning back now."

Through much of your Journey, the Ghost Host will not only be your tour guide, but will also fulfill the dual roles of herald and mentor, announcing each new threshold and explaining some of the paranormal activity you will encounter as you penetrate ever deeper into this supernatural realm. However, here in the Portrait Chamber, he is apparently getting a mischievous kick observing your "cadaverous pallor" as you begin to "...sense a disquieting metamorphosis." But it's not your imagination; the entire room really *is* stretching—including the paintings of several previous guests "...as they appeared in the their corruptible, mortal state."

The stretching gag requires no further narration, setting the tone of morbid silliness that will infuse much of the remainder of your Journey. And now your Ghost Host is cheerfully pointing out that, "This chamber has no windows and no doors...which leaves you with this chilling challenge: to find a way out!" And so you are assigned your first test on the Road of Trials.

Before you can ponder your next move, the gargoyle lamps are suddenly extinguished as a flash of lightning reveals the gruesome sight of the Ghost Host's decaying corpse hanging from the cupola rafters, which have suddenly become visible through the formerly opaque chamber ceiling. A clap of thunder and a bloodcurdling scream complete the effect. When the lights return a moment later, you notice that one of the walls has somehow vanished, allowing you and your fellow adventurers to exit the chamber.

Though you are only at the beginning of your Haunted Mansion tour, you are already becoming acquainted with some of the peculiarities of the otherworldly realm inside this place. First, you are beginning to realize that, in this Special World, things are seldom what they seem at first. Going forward, you can be sure that your expectations (based, reasonably enough, on your experiences in the Ordinary World) will be upended again and again. You are also starting to sense that this house possesses a personality of its own—one with a twisted sense of humor.

Now, as you emerge from the Portrait Chamber, you notice that the Ghost Host's claim that "There's no turning back now" is not quite true. For just outside the chamber is a doorway with a sign: "Full of fear? Exit here." If you belatedly decide to refuse your Call to Adventure, this is your opportunity to make a last-minute escape back to the friendly, familiar environs of Liberty Square. But it's going to take a lot more than a stretching room and a swinging corpse to discourage you from continuing your Journey. And so you bypass the "chicken exit" and instead follow your compatriots into a gloomy corridor where, in the words of the Ghost Host, "...a carriage approaches to carry you into the boundless realm of the supernatural." With its dim, cobwebbed draped chandeliers, its skull-like wall carvings, and its bat-topped queue stanchions, this space turns out to be the creepiest one you've encountered so far on your Journey, with a brain script that clearly communicates "death and decay."

Your carriage, of course, turns out to be a Doom Buggy—a ride vehicle painted a fashionably funereal shade of black, matching the tone of the humor you'll be encountering through the remainder of your Journey. Moments after you step aboard, you cross the first of several shadowy thresholds awaiting you beyond. This one leads to the Portrait Corridor, where flashes of lightning expose the secret monsters lurking within as an angelic young woman turns out to be a horrifying medusa, and a regal knight on a handsome steed is revealed to be a hideous ghoul astride a skeletal horse. It's a continuation of the transformation theme that began in the foyer. But these portraits also hint at the idea that each of us has a private, hidden self, concealed behind the public selves we display to the world. Just as the well-manicured grounds and pristine exterior of the Haunted Mansion conceal a dark, sinister world within, each of us must ultimately acknowledge and deal with the dark inner forces of our own self-doubt, guilt, anger, resentment, jealousy, hubris, or other negative emotions that hold us back and threaten to derail our own life Journeys.

Passing beneath an archway, you enter the Mansion's dimly lit library, which the Ghost Host explains, "…is well-stocked with priceless first editions; only ghost stories, of course." A bookcase ladder moves on its own while an apparently empty rocking chair rocks back and forth and books slide in and out of their places on the dusty bookshelves. Even the marble busts seem endowed with some sort of life force as they shift their gaze to follow your Doom Buggy's motion from their bookcase perches.

It seems some of the Mansion's resident spirits are present, yet you are unable to directly see them, as you are not yet attuned to the spiritual frequencies of this ghostly Special World. Your ever-helpful Ghost Host has a quick remedy however, explaining, "…we have 999 happy haunts here, but there's room for a thousand. Any volunteers, hmmm?" It is perhaps the strangest and most macabre Call to Adventure you will find anywhere in the Disney theme parks. And as if to assure you that he's serious, the Ghost Host adds, "If you should decide to join us, final arrangements may be made at the end of the tour…" Nevertheless, this is one Call to Adventure you should probably pass up.

Next, you enter the Music Room where moonlight streaming through the large windows reveals the shadow of an otherwise invisible pianist, pounding out chords on a dusty old piano. This shadow, according to Imagineering sources, belongs to the Ghost Host, though it's never stated anywhere in the attraction. In fact, this particular scene is presented without any narration at all. In any case, you can only perceive the figure's ghostly presence implicitly as you are still developing the mental skills you will need to directly visualize the Mansion's spectral inhabitants.

Leaving the music room, your Doom Buggy ascends through a chamber where staircases surround you at impossible angles while glowing green footprints appear on the steps. The deeper you penetrate into the mansion, the more you appreciate how far the rules of this Special World depart from those of the Ordinary World. The strange staircase drives home the extent to which your familiar sense of "reality" has been literally turned upside down.

Arriving at the top of the staircases, you notice malevolent-looking eyes scowling at you from the deep shadows. As you move into a gloomy corridor, the eyes eventually merge into the pattern of the creepy wallpaper. Next, you pass a parlor, where a suit of medieval armor and an easy chair decorated with a spooky, abstract face seem to be watching your every move. Nearby, a flickering candelabrum floats eerily in mid-air in a seemingly endless hallway. The candelabrum is not just another uncanny phenomenon; it's also a signal, a beacon. Someone—or more likely some*thing*—is beckoning you to follow. For now, you decline this new Call to Adventure as your Doom Buggy carries you past the corridor and into the next room. Yet the floating candelabrum implies that, for the first time, one of the residents of this peculiar world (other than your Ghost Host) is making at least a token effort to reach out to you.

Now your Doom Buggy rotates around to face backward as you enter the Mansion's conservatory, where dead flowers surround a coffin occupying the center of the room. A raven is perched atop a wreath featuring a banner that reads: "Farewell." However, the eulogies may be premature, as the coffin's occupant is desperately trying to pry the lid open from within, his gnarled hands illuminated by a sickly green light that spills out of the sarcophagus. "All our guests have been dying to meet you," says the voice of the Ghost Host, dripping with sarcasm. "This one can hardly contain himself."

Does the fact that you can clearly see the coffin's occupant (or at least his hands) mean that you have suddenly graduated to the rank of "ghost whisperer" and are now able to visualize the Mansion's spectral inhabitants? Sorry, not really. The hands are visible to you because this is not a spirit at all, but merely an "undead" corpse—or maybe even a still-living individual reluctantly awaiting a premature burial. But rest assured, you will be able to directly perceive the "happy haunts" with your own eyes...though you are not there yet.

And what of the raven on the wreath? As you may have already guessed, the dark, menacing creature is more than mere decoration. The raven, in fact, has a long mythological pedigree. In Norse mythology, the father god Odin has two ravens—Huginn and Muninn—that serve as feathered reconnaissance drones, relaying news to him of everything that happens in Midgard (Middle Earth, the human domain). In other words, Odin's two ravens provide a means of communication between the mortal world and the supernatural realm of the Norse gods. The raven is also a major part of the creation myth of the indigenous peoples of the Pacific Northwest Coast, who also consider the bird to be a trickster god. And most famously, the title figure of Edgar Alan Poe's unnerving 1845 poem "The Raven" plays the role of a supernatural messenger, whose repeated utterance of a single enigmatic word—"Nevermore"—is laden with meaning for the poem's narrator. And so, given its strong symbolic connection with the world beyond, it should hardly come as a surprise that you will be meeting the Mansion raven three more times before your Journey has ended.

The mystical forces flowing through the Mansion now propel your Doom Buggy into a corridor lined with heavy doors. And whoever—or *whatever*—is on the other side of those doors seems anxious to make a grand entrance on your side. Doorknobs twist and doorknockers pound while grunts, growls, and snarls issue from within. A pair of skeletal hands can even be seen pressing one door outward. Fortunately, as your Ghost Host remarks, "They all seem to be having trouble getting through."

The Corridor of Doors (WDI's internal name for this scene) might as well be known as the Corridor of Thresholds. Each one presumably leads into some other part of the Haunted Mansion's Special World. But in this case, the beings on the other side would rather cross over to your side of the threshold. Which just goes to remind you that threshold crossings can work in both directions.

Just beyond the Corridor of Doors, you pass through the Clock Hall, which features a single grandfather clock. A pair of skeletal fingers that serve as the hour and minute hands rapidly spin counter-clockwise, striking the 13th hour every few seconds. At the same time, the shadow of a sinister claw sweeps across the clock's demonic features. The creepy scene serves to reinforce the strangeness of this Special World, reminding you (as if you needed further prompting) that the rules of your familiar, Ordinary World do not apply in this ghostly place.

"Perhaps Madame Leota can establish contact," suggests the Ghost Host as you enter the Séance Circle. "She has a remarkable head for materializing the disembodied." Indeed, you are fascinated by the sight of Madame Leota's luminescent noggin suspended inside a crystal ball, which floats preternaturally above the séance table. The raven from the conservatory, meanwhile, now perches on the back of the chair behind the table, its presence here reinforcing its mythic reputation as a supernatural messenger.

You have caught Madame Leota in the midst of an incantation as she summons the spirits into the visible world, intoning, "Serpents and spiders, tail of a rat—call in the spirits, wherever they're at!" Musical instruments float through the air, responding to her spell, while a formless green apparition traces a phosphorescent trail in the surrounding darkness.

As the medium that establishes contact between you and the spirit world, Madame Leota fulfills the herald archetype, beckoning the Mansion's ghostly residents to reveal themselves. At the same time, she acts as a threshold guardian, regulating the flow of spiritual energy between the dimensions. However, at this point in your Journey, you have undergone your own sensory transformation. Whether you are aware of it or not, the prior chambers you encountered during your tour, with their "wall-to-wall creeps, and hot and cold running chills," were all tests along the mythic Road of Trials. The fact that you (presumably) endured the succession of frights without freaking out has proved your worthiness. And now you are about to collect your Reward.

"The happy haunts have received your sympathetic vibrations and are beginning to materialize," announces your Ghost Host as your Doom Buggy carries you into the Grand Hall, where the Mansion's residents are "...assembling for a swinging wake..." This announcement marks a turning point in your relationship with the Mansion's resident ghosts. They have obviously undergone a transformation, transitioning into a state visible to your mortal eyes. But that transition comes as the direct result of your own metamorphosis, which has enabled you to project your "sympathetic vibrations" into the abode of the dead.

The "swinging wake" proves to be just as rowdy as advertised, with dozens of translucent apparitions waltzing, cavorting drunkenly, swinging from the chandeliers, dueling, and partying themselves silly while even more spooks pour through the ballroom door—all to the tune of "Grim Grinning Ghosts" performed on a ghoulish pipe organ by an equally ghoulish organist. You can now say, with a straight face, "I see dead people."

The festive mood takes a dark turn as your Doom Buggy is unceremoniously diverted to the attic, where a dirge-like piano version of Wagner's Wedding March (AKA "Here Comes the Bride") wafts through the space. You then pass a series of wedding portraits, each one featuring the same bride but a different groom. And in each portrait, the groom's head vanishes before your eyes. Soon you encounter the blushing bride herself—a smiling, wraith-like presence. "I do," she says repeatedly in a slow, menacing voice as a gleaming hatchet materializes in her clasped hands. The implication is clear: this is the girl your mother always warned you about.

In mythic tales, a wedding generally signifies a major milestone in the hero's Journey toward maturity. However, if the hero is not ready for the responsibilities of adulthood, tragedy can ensue—as appears to be the case here. Appropriately, the (literal) beating heart of that tragedy has been hidden away here in the attic, which turns out to be the Inmost Cave of your Hero's Journey, and this encounter is your Supreme Ordeal. Moreover, though the Haunted Mansion storyline is deliberately vague on the subject, it's entirely possible that the hatchet-wielding "black widow" bride may be the epicenter of all the supernatural activities that have taken over the Mansion, with her matrimonial murder spree providing the trigger event that attracted the 998 other happy haunts inhabiting this place. As such, the bride, despite her angelic glow, is actually the shadow archetype in your adventure—a literal *femme fatale,* as well as a shape-shifter and trickster.

As though sensing your unease in the murderous bride's presence, your Doom Buggy hastily transports you out of her vicinity via the most direct means possible: by diving directly out the attic window...and into the Mansion's very unusual graveyard. You are now commencing the Return movement of your Journey, and like many mythic heroes, you briefly "taste death" as your Doom Buggy descends in reverse, making it feel as though you are being laid to rest in an open grave. Meanwhile, the Mansion raven, with its glowing red eyes, watches attentively from the branch of a gnarled old tree.

Nearby, wispy ghosts fly up out of their graves and into the inky night sky, while the caretaker and his emaciated hound stand nearly petrified with fear in front of the cemetery gate. Do they share your newfound ability to visualize the Mansion's happy haunts? Or is it the sudden sight of *you* that has them so terrified? It's anyone's guess. Meanwhile, an upbeat jazz-inflected rendition of "Grim Grinning Ghosts" lilts through the night air, performed by a graveyard ensemble, including a quintet of harmonizing headstones. Ghastly ghouls pop up on either side of your Doom Buggy, while a stout opera diva, a decapitated knight, a lively mummy, and an ethereal cast of other grim grinning ghosts have "...come out to socialize."

The musical number serves as a cheekily cheery send-off as the Return movement continues and you approach a new threshold: a stone archway that leads to the Mansion's shadowy stone crypt. The red-eyed raven joins you one last time, glaring down at you from its perch atop the arch. As the Mansion's unofficial supernatural messenger, the raven's appearance no doubt heralds a new development in your adventure. Perhaps the bird is here to remind you of the fact that the Return movement of the Hero's Journey is often fraught with new perils for the hero.

But what is the nature of this latest menace? "There's a little matter I forgot to mention," offers the voice of the Ghost Host. "Beware of hitchhiking ghosts!" By this time, of course, it's far too late for the warning to be of any value. In any case, the otherworldly forces that have been steering your Doom Buggy all along are still in control, leaving you no choice in your destiny. And so the three ghostly hitchhikers[38] now come into view, and they seem unlikely to take "No! *Please!* For pity's sake, stay away from me! *NOOOO!!!*" for an answer.

Moments later, you are passing a long wall of mirrors, by which point one of the three hitchhikers has already joined you in your vehicle to fulfill its role as a certified trickster archetype. Catching your reflections, you watch with amused disbelief as the hitchhiker proceeds to interact with you in fiendishly silly ways—swapping your head with his own, popping your noggin like a balloon, and playing other literal head games with you. "They have selected you to fill our quota," the Ghost Host informs you, "and they'll haunt you until you return!"

With this scene, your assimilation into the Special World of the Haunted Mansion is now complete. You are not only able to see the happy haunts; now you are actually, (meta)physically interacting with them...and vice-versa. But the hitchhiking ghosts serve another function. Mythic heroes often return from their Journeys in the Special World with a boon: a healing elixir, a magical ring, a miraculous

---

[38] Affectionately nicknamed Phineas, Ezra, and Gus, the three hitchhiking ghosts have become the semi-official mascots of the Haunted Mansion.

sword, or some other souvenir of their adventures. Your token souvenir? A hitchhiking ghost. Mazel tov.

Finally, as your Doom Buggy nears the unload area, a miniature spirit nicknamed "Little Leota" bids you farewell from a shelf overlooking the ride path and urges you to "Hurry *baaack*. Be sure to bring your death certificate if you decide to join us." You then exit your Doom Buggy onto a moving belt, which conveys you to the exit.

Yet your adventures in the Special World are not quite over yet. For you must now pass through the Mansion's outdoor mausoleum, where you are serenaded by an *a capella* rendition of "Grim Grinning Ghosts" performed as a Gregorian chant. The inscriptions on the vaults continue in the style of the morbidly amusing epitaphs you viewed in the front cemetery, including several horrifying puns. Then, if you glance up at the hillside as you exit the mausoleum, you'll even catch a glimpse of a fenced off pet cemetery. Finally, you again pass the black hearse with its invisible horse before you arrive back in the relative Ordinary World of Liberty Square.

The mausoleum experience is part of your transition back to that Ordinary World. Once you are beyond the mystical influence of the Haunted Mansion, you are (presumably) no longer able to "see dead people." That ability has subsided—at least until you "hurry *baaack*," (unless you pay a visit to the residents of the nearby Hall of Presidents, most of whom long ago shuffled off their mortal coils). But your memory of the experience remains, and your assumptions about the spirit world may never be the same. After all, "There's no turning back now!"

BIBLIOGRAPHY

Joseph Campbell and the Power of Myth. PBS, 1988. TV broadcast.

Campbell, Joseph. *The Hero with a Thousand Faces.* Princeton, NJ: Princeton UP, 1972. Print.

Campbell, Joseph, with Moyers, Bill. *The Power of Myth.* New York, Doubleday, 1988. Print.

Wright, Alex. *The Imagineering Field Guide to Epcot.* New York, Disney Editions, 2006. Print.

Kurtti, Jeff. *Walt Disney's Imagineering Legends and the Genesis of the Disney Theme Park.* New York, Disney Editions, 2008. Print.

Malmberg, Melody. *Walt Disney Imagineering: A Behind the Dreams Look at Making MORE Magic Real.* New York: Disney Editions, 2010. Print.

Hench, John, and Peggy van Pelt. *Designing Disney: Imagineering and the Art of the Show.* New York, Disney Editions, 2003. Print.

Marling, Karal Ann. *Designing Disney's Theme Parks: The Architecture of Reassurance.* Paris, Flammarion, 1997. Print.

Bettelheim, Bruno. *The Uses of Enchantment: The Meaning and Importance of Fairy Tales.* New York: Vintage, 1977. Print.

Henderson, Mary S. *Star Wars: The Magic of Myth.* New York: Bantam, 1997. Print.

Vogler, Christopher. *The Writer's Journey: Mythic Structure for Writers.* Studio City, CA: M. Wiese Productions, 1998. Print.

Mikunda, Christian. *The Art of Business Entertainment – 2nd Edition.* Econ Varlag, Germany, 1997. Print.

Gennawey, Sam. *Walt and the Promise of Progress City*. Pike Road, AL: Ayefour, 2011. Print.

"Epcot Film - The Original 'Epcot' Project." *Epcot Film - The Original 'Epcot' Project*. N.p., n.d. Web. 13 May 2013. <https://sites.google.com/site/theoriginalepcot/the-epcot-film-video>.

Thomas, Frank, and Ollie Johnston. *Disney Animation: The Illusion of Life*. New York: Abbeville, 1981. Print.

Bulfinch, Thomas, and Robert Graves. *Bulfinch's Mythology: The Age of Fable*. Garden City, NY: Doubleday, 1968. Print.

Beard, Richard R., and Walt Disney. *Walt Disney's EPCOT Center: Creating the New World of Tomorrow*. New York: H.N. Abrams, 1982. Print.

"Circle Symbol Meaning." *Circle Symbol Meaning*. N.p., n.d. Web. 04 Apr. 2013. <http://www.whats-your-sign.com/circle-symbol-meaning.html>.

Thomas, Bob. *Disney's Art of Animation: From Mickey Mouse to Beauty and the Beast*. New York: Hyperion, 1991. Print.

"The Carousel of Progress Cast." *(Korkis Korner) by Jim Korkis*. N.p., n.d. Web. 07 Apr. 2013. <http://www.mouseplanet.com/9835/The_Carousel_of_Progress_Cast>.

Fergus-Jean, Elizabeth. "LABYRINTH: A Metaphor for Transformation." *Labrinth Paper*. N.p., n.d. Web. 08 Apr. 2013. <http://www.fergusjean.com/labyrinth_p1.htm>.

Surrell, Jason. *The Disney Mountains: Imagineering at Its Peak*. New York: Disney Editions, 2007. Print.

"Sacred Places: Mountains and the Sacred." *Sacred Places: Mountains and the Sacred*. N.p., n.d. Web. 17 Apr. 2013. <http://witcombe.sbc.edu/sacredplaces/mountains.html>.

"Himalayas: Abode of Gods." *About.com Hinduism*. N.p., n.d. Web. 17 Apr. 2013. <http://hinduism.about.com/od/temples/a/himalayas.htm>.

"Sacred Places: Trees and the Sacred." *Sacred Places: Trees and the Sacred*. N.p., n.d. Web. 23 Apr. 2013. <http://witcombe.sbc.edu/sacredplaces/trees.html>.

"Sacred Places: Water and the Sacred." *Sacred Places: Water and the Sacred*. N.p., n.d. Web. 23 Apr. 2013. <http://witcombe.sbc.edu/sacredplaces/water.html>.

"Sacred Rivers of India." *Sacred Rivers of India*. ENVIS Centre on Conservation of Ecological Heritage and Sacred Sites in India, n.d. Web. 23 Apr. 2013. <http://www.ecoheritage.cpreec.org/innerpageof.php?$mFJ yBfKPkE8>.

Wright, Alex. *The Imagineering Field Guide to Disney's Animal Kingdom at Walt Disney World: An Imagineer's-eye Tour*. New York: Disney Editions, 2007. Print.

Wright, Alex. *The Imagineering Field Guide to Disneyland: An Imagineer's-eye Tour*. New York: Disney Editions, 2008. Print.

"Myths Encyclopedia." *Animals in Mythology*. N.p., n.d. Web. 30 Apr. 2013. <http://www.mythencyclopedia.com/Am-Ar/Animals-in-Mythology.html>.

Wallace, Aaron. *The Thinking Fan's Guide to Walt Disney World*. Branford, CT: Intrepid Traveler, 2013. Print.

"Archetypes." *About.com Psychology*. N.p., n.d. Web. 12 May 2013. <http://psychology.about.com/od/personalitydevelopment/t p/archetypes.htm>.

"Psychology and Fairy Tales: By Carrie Hughes." *Psychology and Fairy Tales: By Carrie Hughes*. N.p., n.d. Web. 11 May 2013.

<http://www.mccarter.org/Education/secretinthewings/page 16.htm>.

"Walt Disney and Fairytales." *Walt Disney and Fairytales.* N.p., n.d. Web. 11 May 2013. <http://www.oocities.org/d-patanella/disfai.html>.

Campbell, Joseph. *Myths to Live By.* New York: Viking, 1972. Print.

Barnes, Brooks. "Disney Tackles Major Theme Park Problem: Lines." *The New York Times.* The New York Times, 27 Dec. 2010. Web. 22 May 2013. <http://www.nytimes.com/2010/12/28/business/media/28disney.html?_r=0 >.

"Rocket to the Moon at Yesterland." *Rocket to the Moon at Yesterland.* N.p., n.d. Web. 11 Sept. 2013. <http://www.yesterland.com/moonrocket.html>

Champlin, Charles. *George Lucas: The Creative Impulse,* New York: Harry N. Abrams, Inc., 1992

"THE WALT DISNEY COMPANY COMPLETES LUCASFILM ACQUISITION. "*The Walt Disney Company.* N.p., n.d. Web. 26 May 2013. <http://thewaltdisneycompany.com/disney-news/press-releases/2012/12/walt-disney-company-completes-lucasfilm-acquisition>.

"TheRaider.net - Indiana Jones News, Info and Fan Community." *TheRaider.net - Indiana Jones News, Info and Fan Community.* N.p., n.d. Web. 29 May 2013. <http://www.theraider.net/>.

"MYTHOLOGY OF BEES HONEY." *MYTHOLOGY OF BEES HONEY.* N.p., n.d. Web. 12 June 2013. <http://lunedemiel.tm.fr/anglais/06.htm>.

"The History Place - Great Speeches Collection: John F. Kennedy Speech "We Choose to Go to the Moon..."" *The History Place - Great Speeches Collection: John F. Kennedy Speech "We Choose to Go to the Moon..."* N.p., n.d. Web. 13 May 2013. <http://www.historyplace.com/speeches/jfk-space.htm>.

Writer, Brady MacDonald | Los Angeles Times Staff. "Scene-by-scene Preview: Radiator Springs Racers at Disney California Adventure." *Los Angeles Times*. Los Angeles Times, 17 Oct. 2011. Web. 04 July 2013. <http://articles.latimes.com/2011/oct/17/news/la-trb-radiator-springs-racers-disney-10201117>.

"Step Inside Radiator Springs At Cars Land In Disney California Adventure – Part 7." N.p., n.d. Web. 04 July 2013. <http://damouse.com/2012/06/13/step-inside-radiator-springs-at-cars-land-in-disney-california-adventure-part-7/>.

"Dead Men... TELL NO TALES!" *Dead Men... TELL NO TALES!* N.p., n.d. Web. 04 Aug. 2013. <http://www.tellnotales.com/home.php>.

Surrell, Jason. *Pirates of the Caribbean: From the Magic Kingdom to the Movies.* New York: Disney Editions, 2005. Print.

"Symbolic Meanings Blog by Avia Venefica." *Symbolic Meanings Blog by Avia Venefica RSS.* N.p., n.d. Web. 04 Aug. 2013. <http://www.symbolic-meanings.com/2009/10/07/symbolic-meaning-of-gold/>.

Surrell, Jason. *The Haunted Mansion: From the Magic Kingdom to the Movies.* New York: Disney Editions, 2003. Print.

"DoomBuggies Explore the History and Marvel at the Mystery of Disney's Haunted Mansion Attractions!" *DoomBuggies Explore the History and Marvel at the Mystery of Disney's Haunted Mansion Attractions!* N.p.,

n.d. Web. 30 Aug. 2013. <
http://www.doombuggies.com/myths2.php>

ACKNOWLEDGEMENTS

NO ONE UNDERTAKES HIS OR HER PERSONAL HERO'S JOURNEY ALONE. In my case, the Journey that led to the creation of this book began long before I ever typed the first words. Along the way, I was constantly propelled forward and encouraged in my quest by many allies.

It began with my parents, Merton and Charney Berger, who took my two brothers and me to Walt Disney World for the first time when I was 12 years old. That first visit kicked off my Disney theme park obsession, which endures to this day. I owe them my eternal gratitude for encouraging my obsession and for guiding me to channel it into an eventual career as an attraction show writer, designer, and creative consultant. I only wish everyone could be lucky enough to have such supportive parents.

I also owe my thanks to a long line of teachers through every stage of my education, who were able to find potential in me even when I couldn't. Foremost among them was Janet Atwood, who stoked my love of writing during my high school years with her precision blend of encouragement, praise, and constructive criticism. She was my original mentor.

More recently, I am grateful for the many attraction design professionals who have given me the opportunity to pursue my show writing career and to work on so many wonderful projects over the years. They include Bill Coan and the team at ITEC Entertainment Corporation, Anthony Esparza and Merrill Puckett Miller of Herschend Family Entertainment, Colette Piceau of It Ain't Shakespeare, Bob Salmon of Ride The Ducks International, Trevor Bryant of BB Productions, and many others at Universal Creative, Walt Disney Imagineering, and a long list of other themed design organizations.

Thanks also to Jim Hill for giving me a forum for my original "Mything in Action" articles on his entertainment blog JimHillMedia.com; to Sam Gennawey for his encouragement and specific advice; and to my mother-in-law Sheila Phillips for her invaluable help in proofreading the first-draft manuscript. And thanks to my beautiful son Micah, who has given me the opportunity to experience the Disney parks anew through his young eyes and his boundless sense of wonder.

Finally, my everlasting gratitude to my beloved wife Julia, who not only puts up with my theme park obsession every day, but often shares in it. She is the one who gave me the impetus to finally write this book after years of false starts. She then provided crucial feedback and patiently served as my creative sounding board whenever needed (even late at night). Throughout the Journey, she never failed to rekindle my enthusiasm whenever I felt my motivation flagging. So it is no exaggeration when I say I never could have written this book without her.

ADAM M. BERGER IS PRESIDENT AND SENIOR SHOW WRITER at
Berger Creative Associates, Inc., an Orlando, Florida-based
creative writing and consulting firm serving the themed
entertainment and attraction design industry. His credits
include projects for Dollywood, Disney Event Productions,
Kennedy Space Center, Nickelodeon Recreation, Paramount
Parks, Ride The Ducks, SeaWorld, Silver Dollar City, Six
Flags, Universal Studios Florida, Walt Disney Imagineering,
and many others. Adam's observations about mythic
storytelling and the Hero's Journey in contemporary pop
culture and entertainment can be found at:

www.themythinglink.com

15206291R00164

Made in the USA
Middletown, DE
27 October 2014